KU-253-206

# THE TIMES

# HOW TO CRACK CRYPTIC CROSSWORDS

## Tim Moorey

Includes 24 practice puzzles from the *Sun*, *Daily Mail*, *The Times*, *The Sunday Times*, *Daily Telegraph*, *Sunday Telegraph*, *Financial Times*, *Guardian*, *Independent on Sunday*, *Observer*, *Oldie*, *The Week* and *Oxford Times*

HarperCollins Publishers
Westerhill Road
Bishopbriggs
Glasgow
G64 2QT

www.harpercollins.co.uk

HarperCollins*Publishers*
Macken House, 39/40 Mayor Street Upper
Dublin1, D01 C9W8, Ireland

Copyright © Tim Moorey 2018

Puzzles © *Daily Mail*, *Daily Telegraph*, *Sunday Telegraph*

*The Times*® is a registered trademark of Times Newspapers Limited

ISBN 978-0-00-828557-9

10

Layout by Susie Bell – www.f-12.co.uk

Printed and bound in the UK using 100% renewable electricity at CPI Group (UK) Ltd

All rights reserved. No part of this book may be reproduced, stored in a retrieval system, or transmitted in any form or by any means, electronic, mechanical, photocopying, recording or otherwise, without the prior permission in writing of the Publisher. This book is sold subject to the conditions that it shall not, by way of trade or otherwise, be lent, re-sold, hired out or otherwise circulated without the Publisher's prior consent in any form of binding or cover other than that in which it is published and without a similar condition including this condition being imposed on the subsequent purchaser.

The contents of this publication are believed correct at the time of printing. Nevertheless the publisher can accept no responsibility for errors or omissions, changes in the detail given or for any expense or loss thereby caused.

A catalogue record for this book is available from the British Library.

If you would like to comment on any aspect of this book, please contact us at the given address or online via email: puzzles@harpercollins.co.uk

facebook.com/collinsdictionary

@collinsdict

MIX
Paper | Supporting responsible forestry
FSC™ C007454

This book is produced from independently certified FSC™ paper to ensure responsible forest management.

For more information visit: www.harpercollins.co.uk/green

# Contents

To my dear Pam, partner for over 50 years without whose...
(her no-nonsense modesty prevented me from completing this!)

# Introduction

*"In Victorian times a popular game was Magic Square... In 1913 Arthur Wynne was given the task of devising a new puzzle for the World. He adapted the magic square by blackening in some squares and criss-crossing the words. Thus was the first ever crossword puzzle created."*

The Advertiser, Adelaide

## What's the aim of this book?

I hope to show that, for any daily or weekly crossword puzzle, it is possible to improve your solving skills substantially by the study and application of a few straightforward rules and techniques.

## So, is this book only for beginners?

Not at all, it is also for anyone wanting to master crossword puzzles so he or she isn't regularly left with unfinished clues before the next day's newspaper arrives. It may also appeal to others happy to enjoy many first-rate clues and practice puzzles from the sources that abound in the book.

## Is there a typical person who might benefit?

Whilst I wouldn't wish to deter others, the person who enjoys a daily struggle with a Quick (non-cryptic) crossword appearing in nearly every newspaper, is an ideal recruit to the world of cryptics. He or she will soon find that they are being given only one way of cracking a clue ie by definition only; cryptics more often than not have two ways, sometimes more, and take full advantage of the delights and richness of the English language.

## What are my qualifications?

My experience as:

1. A (not very fast) solver of crosswords for over 60 years, starting with the *London Evening News*, followed by the *Radio Times* and the *News Chronicle*.

2. A crossword setter whose first crossword was published in the *Evening News* in 1956.
3. Author of *How to Master The Times Crossword* (HarperCollins 2008) which explained cryptic clues in innovative charts that have been well received and are again used in this book.
4. A tutor of crossword workshops around the country for adults and children for over 20 years.

## Is this then an update of *How to Master The Times Crossword*?

Feedback on this first book showed that it proved useful for solving crosswords other than·*The Times*. This encouraged me to write a generic book, *How to Crack Cryptic Crosswords* in 2014, applicable to just about any crossword with puzzles and clues from a variety of sources, not only *The Times*.

## Is this then an update of *How to Crack Cryptic Crosswords*?

Yes it is, for the following reasons:

- Practice being crucial, to give more solving opportunity via 24 all new puzzles from a variety of publications. Each is partnered by detailed explanations as to why answers are what they are;
- It contains many new example clues explaining the basics even more clearly than before and uses the same explanatory diagrams that proved popular in my earlier books;
- The update has been written after gaining from my workshops lots more experience of what new solvers find most helpful. To that end, many new clues should seem easier than their predecessors;
- The launch of the Times Quick Cryptic. Smaller and easier than the main Times Crossword, this has proved to be an excellent puzzle for teaching newcomers and is used extensively in the present update;
- There are many new internet sites and media outlets for cryptics.

My hope is that these features provide good reason for total newcomers and my previous readers of both books to enjoy and learn from this update.

## Are there rules and conventions applying to all cryptic crosswords?

It surprises people to hear that there are, as set down by Ximenes (see box) and they are followed to a large extent by the clue writers and crossword setters whose work appears here.

## So which crosswords are not covered?

Barred crosswords such as Mephisto (*Sunday Times*), Azed (*Observer*), the Inquisitor (*the i*), Beelzebub (the *Independent on Sunday*), Enigmatic Variations (*Sunday Telegraph*) and the Listener Crossword (in the Saturday *Times*) are not used as examples. Solvers of these puzzles at the top of the difficulty scale are not in need of instruction.

> **XIMENES AND AZED**
> Having taken his name from a Grand Inquisitor in the Spanish Inquisition, Ximenes (Derrick Macnutt), a Marlborough College student and Classics master at Christ's Hospital, was long-term setter of a crossword puzzle in the *Observer*. He is remembered today, not just for his puzzles, but also because he set out fair and consistent principles for cryptic crosswords, design and clues in a ground-breaking 1966 book *Ximenes on the Art of the Crossword*, reissued in 2001. His successor Azed (Jonathan Crowther) and the majority of setters today in national media follow virtually all of what are known as 'Ximenean' principles. See page 109 for more on these.

## What about Jumbo crosswords?

No examples of these puzzles are included on the grounds of space but the clueing and solving principles and practice described are just as relevant to their solvers.

## What's the book's focus?

It's firmly on the solver. The teaching sections have been written after consulting a large number of solver friends, colleagues, acquaintances and workshop students, much of whose experience and techniques are incorporated. To this end, a setter's blog in the previous book is replaced by practice puzzles.

## Are there rules for solving?

No, and I certainly would not wish to be seen as laying rules down. Everyone finds their own way of doing crosswords and my hope is that I help you to find yours. Also I invite you to adopt or reject the tips according to whether they suit you.

One thing I will point out, albeit hesitantly, is that on my workshops, female students tend to be 'instinctive' solvers (initial guess and work out why afterwards) whereas male students tend to be more 'analytical' in their initial solving. But that's naturally not always the case: the key point is that it doesn't matter which type you are.

## How to reinforce the teaching?

I follow the well-established teaching principle that adults learn best by doing, rather than reading or being talked at. So I have included lots of practice clues and puzzles, with detailed explanatory notes setting out the solutions to every practice clue and puzzle. They should leave you in no doubt about why the solutions are what they are, a common frustration for solvers. Finally, a full index is designed to encourage the book's continual use, rather than a book that you read once and then donate to a charity shop.

The practice clues in Chapter 3 come from a variety of sources and many are to savour, as they have been selected as 'The Clue of The Week', a feature of *The Week* magazine for the past 20 years.

## Why do people shy away from cryptics?

There are many fears and misapprehensions about the cryptic crossword, usually displayed at the start of my workshops. It is commonly thought that:

- you require a good knowledge of rare words, literature and the classics;
- clues lead to more than one answer;
- the cryptic is always harder than the Quick, non-cryptic puzzle
- there are no rules;
- you need to have 'that sort of mind'.

I hope by the end of this book to have dispelled, partly or wholly, all of these myths.

## What sort of knowledge is needed?

On my workshops I've discovered that any moderately well-educated person with a love of language and problem-solving, and average general knowledge can complete a cryptic crossword. On these points, Richard Browne, a former *Times* crossword editor, has explained:

'Thirty years ago setters could confidently expect that most solvers would have a reasonable acquaintance with the principal plays of Shakespeare, the main characters and events in the Bible, probably a bit of Milton, a few lyric verses, Dickens perhaps, certainly Sherlock Holmes and some staples of the Victorian nursery such as Lear and Lewis Carroll, and you could confidently clue a word just with a reference. That doesn't work any more, partly because the world has widened up so much.

'We have lots of people in this country now from different backgrounds – India, Africa, America, whatever – who have a different system of education, and of course we have people logging on worldwide to *Times* Online, doing the crossword. So it's a larger and more varied audience – you're no longer talking exclusively to the public-school, Oxbridge types who were the core of your readership 50 or 60 years ago.'

Importantly, these comments apply to most cryptics published today.

## Finally, why do crosswords?

*'I always do the crossword first thing in the morning, to see if I've enough marbles left to make it worth my while getting up.'*
Letter to *The Times* from an elderly reader

There is indeed scientific evidence that tackling a crossword can be good for you. Medical research continues to support the notion that mental exercise from activities such as crosswords is beneficial, especially in later life, and stimulates the brain. A New York neurologist, Doctor Joe Verghese, conducted research in this area for over 21 years and found that those who kept their minds nimble were 75 per cent less likely to develop dementia or Alzheimer's disease.

'Do something that is mentally challenging to you,' he has said. 'It seems that remaining mentally agile makes the brain more healthy and more likely to resist illness, just as physical exercise can protect the body from disease.'

In addition, are crosswords educational? I say yes, in the sense that they undoubtedly can improve your vocabulary and general knowledge.

Incidentally, you can check the number of words in your vocabulary via www.testyourvocab.com, against the average native English speaker's 27,000 words. Maybe one plan is for you to check your score again after you have mastered this book!

It's now time to get stuck into some basics, in which I assume no previous knowledge whatever.

**A CLUE-A-DAY**
Some Indian states have a daily cryptic clue-solving contest for children
– see www.crypticsingh.com/acad

# CROSSWORD BASICS

## 1: Terminology

*"She had another look at* The Times Crossword. *The clues might as well have been written in a foreign language."*
Simon Brett, *The Stabbing in the Stables*

The first three chapters of Part 1 establish the terms used throughout. They are essential reading for beginners, and perhaps also for some seasoned solvers who may have become used to different terminology.

### What is a cryptic clue?

A cryptic clue is a sentence or phrase, involving a degree of deception, making sense and frequently conjuring an image, or triggering thoughts, in its surface reading; but when read in another way can be decoded using a limited number of well-established techniques to give a solution. Thus "cryptic" is used in its meaning of hidden or misleading.

These are the other terms we shall use:

- Answers to **clues**, running across and down are entered into a **grid**, popularly a diagram, which has **across** and **down** empty squares to be filled.
- The grids in the case of the puzzles we are considering here contain black square **blocks**, hence they are seen in **blocked** puzzles.
- The other main type not being considered here has a grid with **bars** rather than blocks, hence the term **barred** puzzles.
- Clue answers are variously called **solutions**, **entries** and indeed **answers**.
- Where a solution letter, or letters, is able to be confirmed by intersecting entries, they are **checked** letters. **Unchecked** letters (**unches** in the trade) are therefore the opposite: the solver has no second way of confirming them.

- The sense conveyed by the initial reading of a clue is the **surface meaning**.
- The person responsible for the crossword is a **setter**; more commonly, but in a term less attractive to most crossword professionals, a **compiler**.
- The term **constructor**, which suits puzzles with difficult-to-build grids, is used in North America.
- The number of letters in a clue solution, always shown at the end of the clue, is termed the **enumeration**.
- Other terms associated with clues such as **wordplay**, **anagram**, **indicator** and **anagram fodder** are explained as we meet them.

For completeness, there is a rarely used crossword term – **light** – whose meaning has fluctuated somewhat from the early days of crosswords but is defined by the *Collins English Dictionary* today as the solution to a clue.

### ARE CRYPTICS EXCLUSIVELY BRITISH?
Commonwealth countries such as Canada, Australia, New Zealand, India, Malaysia, Singapore, Kenya, Malta and South Africa have daily cryptics similar to British ones, as does Ireland. US crosswords are different in that grids are more open and clues are mildly cryptic or straightforward definitions. There are some occasional British-style puzzles in the *New York Times* and elsewhere. Nonetheless the UK can be considered the home of cryptics. For example, *Daily Telegraph* crosswords are syndicated to around 20 countries.

### CROSSWORDS BETTER THAN SEX: DAILY MAIL ONLINE
When a cryptic crossword is solved, the brain releases dopamine, a chemical agent that makes sex, winning and eating more enjoyable.

# 2: Overview of Clues and Indicators

*"The question is," said Alice, "whether you can make words mean so many different things."*
Lewis Carroll, *Through the Looking Glass*

In this chapter I provide a short overview of the basics of clues and how to recognize them. Detailed points on each clue type are the subject of Chapter 3.

## Characteristics of a cryptic clue

We will consider twelve types of cryptic clue, of which the majority conform to the principles contained in this image:

**Cryptic clues (mostly) have two parts**

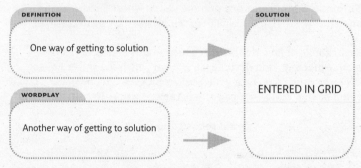

DEFINITION

One way of getting to solution

WORDPLAY

Another way of getting to solution

SOLUTION

ENTERED IN GRID

Either the definition or the wordplay can come first in the clue sentence; and either could be exploited first to obtain the solution. Whichever does come second in your solving order acts as confirmation that you have the correct solution.

Taking each element in turn:

**Definition**: The definition can
- take the form of a word, or words in a phrase
- be an example of the solution (e.g. *fruit* can be defined as *apple, perhaps*)

- be a (misleadingly expressed) synonym of the solution. To this end, definitions are often words that have more than one meaning

**Wordplay**: This is the way to elicit the solution if the definition does not do so. It can be seen as either:
- the letters of the solution needing manipulation in one of several ways to provide another indication of the definition, *or*
- individual word or words in the clue having to be interpreted in a different way from the surface meaning

Perhaps strictly accurately the terms should be **word** and **letterplay** (though not, as an elderly student once stumbled over, "loveplay"!).

**TOP TIP – DEFINITION PLACEMENT**
Beginners find it much easier to decode a cryptic clue when they are told that the **definition** is almost always either at the beginning or end of the clue sentence or phrase.

**Solution**: This can be one or more words whose word-length is shown at the end of the clue in parentheses (the **enumeration**).

An example of how this works is seen in this clue which has a simple juxtaposition of three parts from which the solver has to discover which parts are which before progress can be made. Here it could be that either *find* or *above* is the definition. In fact it is *find*.

### Find record above (8)

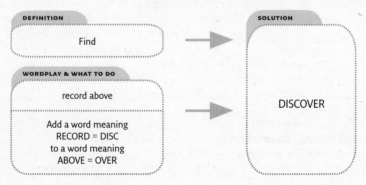

DEFINITION

Find

WORDPLAY & WHAT TO DO

record above

Add a word meaning
RECORD = DISC
to a word meaning
ABOVE = OVER

SOLUTION

DISCOVER

**Linkwords**: Few clues are as straightforward in construction as the previous example and the first mild challenge is that there is often a linkword between the two parts to give the solution. The chart then is:

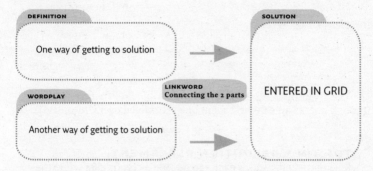

## CRYPTIC CLUES WITH LINKING WORDS

Below is a clue which also starts with the definition but, in addition, has a linkword, one that is commonly used: *from*. The sense conveyed by *from* is that a synonym for church house can be formed from the two parts *earlier* and *years* (if the latter is taken as an abbreviation – more on this later).

### Church house from earlier years (6)

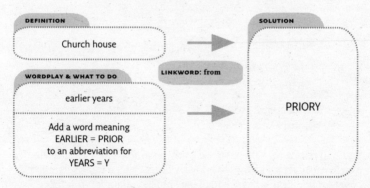

Next is an example in which the definition is the final word in the clue and in which the linkword is *in*, the sense being that the wordplay is *seen in* the solution.

**ADDITIVE CLUE: Keep wine in northern town (9)**

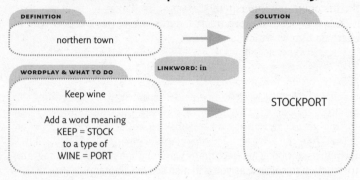

DEFINITION
northern town

SOLUTION
STOCKPORT

LINKWORD: in

WORDPLAY & WHAT TO DO
Keep wine

Add a word meaning
KEEP = STOCK
to a type of
WINE = PORT

As well as linkwords between definition and wordplay, there can also be similar linkage within the wordplay to connect its different parts. Here it is *and*, a simple additive indication. The other linkword *is* indicates that the definition can be formed from the wordplay.

**ADDITIVE CLUE: What babies need is sleep and food (7)**

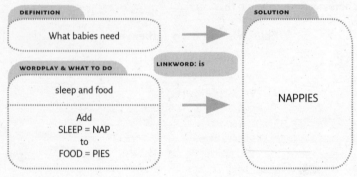

DEFINITION
What babies need

SOLUTION
NAPPIES

LINKWORD: is

WORDPLAY & WHAT TO DO
sleep and food

Add
SLEEP = NAP
to
FOOD = PIES

You will notice that the last two of the example clues are labelled *additive*. In fact all so far have been of this type, a relatively plain construction of A + B = C which we shall consider later in more detail as one of the twelve clue types, dividing these into one group of eight and one group of four. Why split clues into two groups? Because some always contain the means of identifying their type (the **first eight**) and others virtually always do not (the **remaining four**). This distinction is amplified in the section which follows.

## Indicators

At this point, beginners tend to say:

"Yes, I know that there are different types of clue but how on earth do I know which is which?"

The answer is as follows. For the **first group of eight** there is always a signpost to the solution, called the indicator, within the clue sentence. Remember, an indicator is the means of identifying clue types. In Chapter 3 we will consider the specific indicators for the first group of eight clue types. In the example the indicator is *wrong*, showing that this is an **anagram** clue. The concept behind this indicator is that the letters to be mixed are incorrect and must be changed to form the solution. There are many ways of giving the same anagram instruction to solvers, as you will also see in Chapter 3.

**ANAGRAM CLUE: President saw nothing wrong (10)**

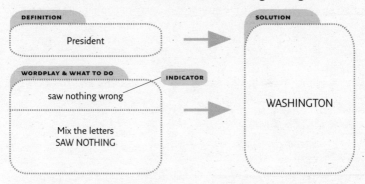

For the **remaining group of four**, it's usually a case of informed guesswork rather than indicators. This may seem unreasonable and impossible for the novice solver but I aim to prove that this is not really the case.

In the meantime, this may be a good time to point out that trial and error and/or inspired guesswork are part and parcel of good solving. This is reinforced by the clueing practice of all good setters whereby the clue type will nearly always become clear on working backwards from the solutions. Indeed, when a solver sees the solution the following day, he or she should only rarely be left thinking (as Ximenes put it):

"I thought of that but I couldn't see how it could be right."

We will now proceed to examine in detail all clue types and their indicators, with one and sometimes two examples of each type.

# 3: Clue Types and Indicators in Detail

*"Give us a kind of clue."* W.S. Gilbert, *Utopia Limited*

Until Chapter 8, we'll keep it simple with regard to clue types.
In later chapters we will see that the clue types can and often do
overlap, involving more than one sort of manipulation of letters or
words within any one clue.

## The first eight clue types

We will now examine each of the eight clue types in detail, together
with their indicators, and offer some example clues. To give yourself
solving practice, you may wish from now on to cover up the bottom
part of the diagram that contains the solution and wordplay.

The first eight types are shown in the circular chart below, and we
shall take each in turn, working clockwise from the top.

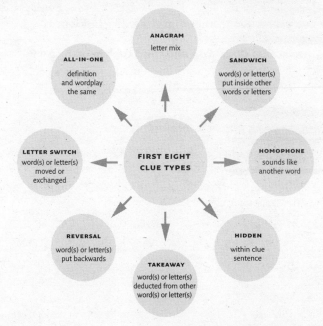

## 1. The anagram clue

An anagram, sometimes termed a **letter mix**, is a rearrangement of letters or words within the clue sentence to form the solution word or words.

The letters to be mixed (the **anagram fodder**) may or may not include an abbreviation, a routine trick for old hands but, as I have observed, a cause of some discomfort for first-timers.

**ANAGRAM CLUE: Mum, listen for a change (6)**

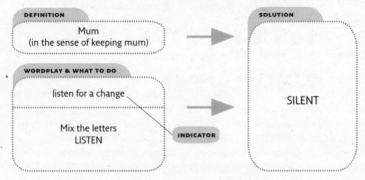

This next example is an **anagram** clue with a **linkword**:

**ANAGRAM CLUE: Fish and chips cooked with lard (9)**

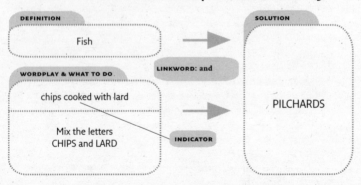

The third example is one wherein the **anagram fodder** goes well with the definition to form a remarkably accurate whole:

**ANAGRAM CLUE: The new stadium designed for a football club (4,3,6)**

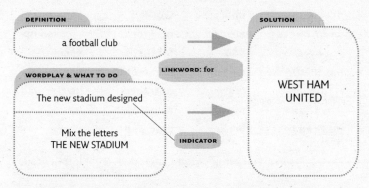

DEFINITION

a football club

SOLUTION

LINKWORD: for

WEST HAM
UNITED

WORDPLAY & WHAT TO DO

The new stadium designed

Mix the letters
THE NEW STADIUM

INDICATOR

*For* is a linkword here in the sense that the wordplay is to be arranged *for* the answer. The essential point for indicators of **anagram** clues is that they show a rearrangement, a disturbance to the natural order or a change to be made. There are very many ways of doing this, some reasonably straightforward but others requiring a stretch of the imagination. For example, words and phrases related to drunkenness and madness have to be taken as involving disturbance so that *stoned, pickled, tight, bananas, nuts, crackers* and *out to lunch* could all be misleading ways to indicate an anagram. I am often asked for a comprehensive list but, because there are so many, unfortunately there is no such list, though the *Chambers Crossword Dictionary* (see page 112) has a large list of anagram and other indicators. The table that follows on the next page is designed to expand on the various categories of rearrangement by giving a few examples of each overleaf:

**TOP TIP - ANAGRAMS**
Early crosswords did not indicate an anagram; solvers were required to guess that a mixture of letters was needed. This is universally regarded as unfair on the solver so that there will always nowadays be an indication of an anagram.

| SOME INDICATORS FOR ANAGRAM CLUES | | | |
|---|---|---|---|
| ARRANGEMENT | sorted | somehow | anyhow |
| REARRANGEMENT | revised | reassembled | resort |
| CHANGE | bursting | out of place | shift |
| DEVELOPMENT | improved | worked | treat |
| WRONGNESS | amiss | in error | messed up |
| STRANGENESS | odd | fantastic | eccentric |
| DRUNKENNESS | smashed | hammered | lit up |
| MADNESS | crazy | outraged | up the wall |
| MOVEMENT | mobile | runs | hit |
| DISTURBANCE OF ORDER | broken | muddled | upset |
| INVOLVEMENT | complicated | tangled | implicated |

## 2. The sandwich clue

A sandwich can be considered as bread outside some filling. Similarly in this clue type, the solution can be built from one part either being put **outside** another part or put **inside** another part.

This is an example of **outside** (with an abbreviation to be made in wordplay):

### SANDWICH CLUE: Simple mug holding one litre (6)

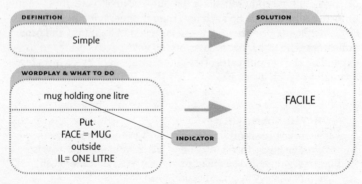

DEFINITION

Simple

SOLUTION

WORDPLAY & WHAT TO DO

mug holding one litre

Put
FACE = MUG
outside
IL = ONE LITRE

INDICATOR

FACILE

This is an example of **inside** with a clear instruction as to what's to be done:

**SANDWICH CLUE: Family member put us in the money (6)**

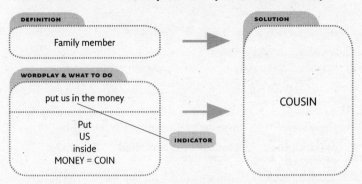

DEFINITION

Family member

WORDPLAY & WHAT TO DO

put us in the money

Put
US
inside
MONEY = COIN

INDICATOR

SOLUTION

COUSIN

## SOME INDICATORS FOR SANDWICH CLUES

| OUTSIDE | | |
|---|---|---|
| contains | clothing | boxing |
| houses | harbours | carries |
| grasping | enclosing | including |
| restrains | protecting | about |

| INSIDE | | |
|---|---|---|
| breaks | cuts | boring |
| piercing | penetrating | fills |
| enters | interrupting | amidst |
| held by | occupies | splitting |

Note that *about* has multiple uses in crosswords (see Chapter 10).

## 3. The homophone clue

In this type, the solution sounds like another word given by the wordplay. The clue is often fairly easy to recognize but it may be harder to find the two words which sound alike.

**HOMOPHONE CLUE: The Speaker's feeble for seven days (4)**

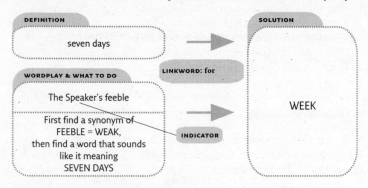

DEFINITION

seven days

LINKWORD: for

WORDPLAY & WHAT TO DO

The Speaker's feeble

First find a synonym of
FEEBLE = WEAK,
then find a word that sounds
like it meaning
SEVEN DAYS

INDICATOR

SOLUTION

WEEK

## Indicators for homophone clues:

Anything which gives an impression of sounding like another word such as *so to speak*, *we hear*, *it's said* acts as an indicator. This extends to what's heard in different real-life situations; for example, at home it could be *on the radio*; in the theatre it could be *to an audience*; in the office it could be *for an auditor*.

## 4. The hidden clue

A hidden clue is arguably the easiest type to solve. That's because the letters to be uncovered require no change: they just need to be dug out of the sentence designed to conceal them. In the first example, the indicator is *inside*:

**HIDDEN CLUE: Parched inside Kalahari desert (4)**

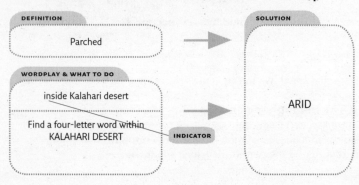

DEFINITION

Parched

WORDPLAY & WHAT TO DO

inside Kalahari desert

Find a four-letter word within
KALAHARI DESERT

INDICATOR

SOLUTION

ARID

**Indicators for hidden clues:**
Commonly *some* (in the sense of a certain part of what follows), *some of*, *partly*, are unique to **hidden** clues; *within*, *amidst*, *holding* and *in* can be either **hidden** or **sandwich** indicators.

A variant of the **hidden** clue is where the letters are concealed at intervals within the wordplay, most commonly odd or even letters. You are asked to extract letters that appear as, say, the first, third and fifth letters in the wordplay section of the clue sentence and ignore the intervening letters. Note that there will never be superfluous words in such a clue sentence, making it easier to be certain which letters are involved in the extraction.

Here is one such clue in which you have to take only the odd letters of *the bar* for the solution.

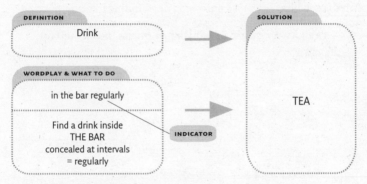

**HIDDEN CLUE: Drink in the bar regularly (3)**

DEFINITION
Drink

WORDPLAY & WHAT TO DO
in the bar regularly

Find a drink inside
THE BAR
concealed at intervals
= regularly

INDICATOR

SOLUTION
TEA

**Some other indicators for hidden-at-intervals clues:**
*Oddly, evenly, ignoring the odds, alternately.*

## 5. The takeaway clue
A **takeaway** clue involves something being deducted from something else. This can be one or more letters or a whole word. In the example below it's one letter, *R*, which is an abbreviation of *right*, and *get* is an instruction to the solver. It should be noted that sometimes you will find abbreviations signposted, e.g. "a small street", more usually not, e.g. "street". You will find in the Appendices a list of those most frequently appearing in crosswords and all of those used in the clues and puzzles of this book.

**TAKEAWAY CLUE: Get employed right away in Surrey town (6)**

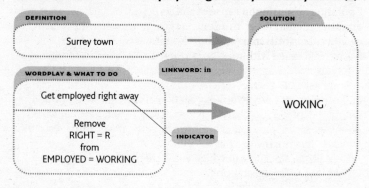

In our second example, it's the last letter that is to be taken away to leave the solution:

**TAKEAWAY CLUE: Silent Disney movie unfinished (4)**

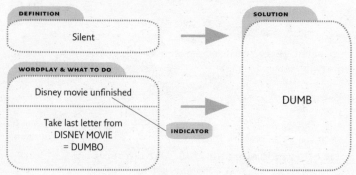

## Indicators for takeaway clues:

These tend to be self-explanatory, such as *reduced, less, extracted,* but, beware, they can be highly misleading, such as *cast* in a clue concerning the theatre, or *shed* in one ostensibly about the garden. Some indicators inform us that a single letter is to be taken away. These include *short, almost, briefly, nearly* and *most of,* all signifying by long-established convention that the final letter of a word is to be removed. There is more on **takeaway** indicators such as *unopened, disheartened, needing no introduction* and *endless* on pages 31–33, which deal with **letter selection** indicators.

## 6. The reversal clue

The whole of a solution can sometimes be reversed to form another entirely different word. In addition, writing some letters backwards or upwards is often part of a clue's wordplay, but for the time being we are concerned with reversal providing the whole of the answer. This is a clue for an across solution:

### REVERSAL CLUE: Knock back beer like a king (5)

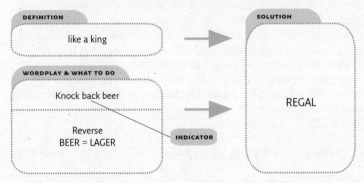

This is a reversal clue for a down solution (see below for an explanation of why this matters):

### REVERSAL CLUE (DOWN): Boat however turned up (3)

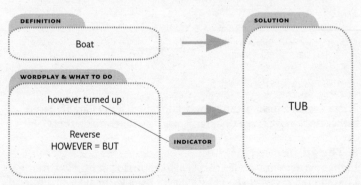

### Indicators for reversal clues:

Anything showing backward movement, e.g. *around, over, back, recalled.*

Do be aware that some **reversal** indicators apply to **down** clues only, reflecting their position in the grid. The example above of a **down** clue uses *turned up* for this purpose; other possibilities are *overturned, raised, up, on the way up* and *served up*.

## 7. The letter switch clue

Where two words differ from each other by one or more letters, this can be exploited by setters so that moving one or more letters produces another word, the solution. Here is an example in which you are instructed to shift *S* for *South* along a word meaning *coast* to produce a fish. You are not told which of the two *s*'s is to be moved but trial and error will eventually show it's the second.

An extra point to be brought out here is that if a pause or comma after the first word is imagined, the instruction should become clearer. This imaginary punctuation effect is common to many crossword clues; see Chapter 4, pages 40–42, for more on this point.

**LETTER SWITCH CLUE: : Fish move south along the coast (3,5)**

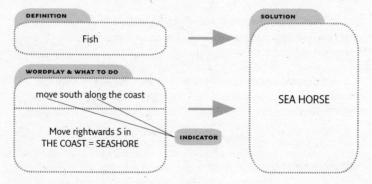

DEFINITION

Fish

WORDPLAY & WHAT TO DO

move south along the coast

Move rightwards S in
THE COAST = SEASHORE

INDICATOR

SOLUTION

SEA HORSE

There is also a form of letter switch in which letters are replaced rather than moved; see Chapter 8, page 71, for more on this.

## 8. The all-in-one clue

In many crossword circles this is also known as **& lit**. However, I have found my workshop participants usually consider this too cryptic a name! It actually means "and is literally so" but people tend to puzzle over that at the expense of understanding the concept.

In fact, it is a simple one that I prefer to call **all-in-one**, which is what it is: the definition and wordplay are combined into one, often shortish sentence which, when decoded, leads to a description of the solution.

**ALL-IN-ONE CLUE: Heads of the several amalgamated Russian states (5)**

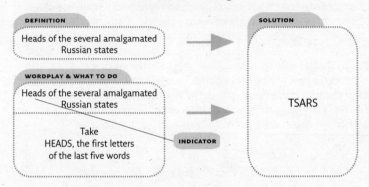

This clue relies on the **letter selection** indicator *heads* (see page 31) to provide the solution. Most of the clueing techniques outlined earlier can be used to make an **all-in-one** clue (see examples in Chapter 8, pages 72–74), always provided that the definition and wordplay are one and the same.

Probably the commonest type is an **all-in-one anagram**, with an anagram as part or all of the wordplay and no extra definition needed because it has been provided by the wordplay. Here is an example:

**ALL-IN-ONE ANAGRAM CLUE: A pot's stirred with one? (8)**

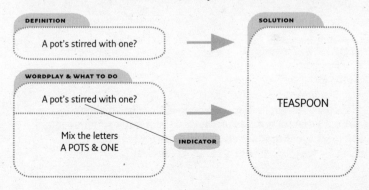

Incidentally, this clue demonstrates how punctuation can give you some help with a clue. The question mark is telling you that a pot isn't necessarily stirred with a spoon but it may be. For examples of when punctuation is not so helpful, see Chapter 4, pages 40-41.

## The remaining four types

Now we will focus on the remaining four clue types. Remember that these four only very rarely include indicators within the clue sentence. Here they are together in one chart from which we will proceed to examine each one in turn, starting at the top and going clockwise.

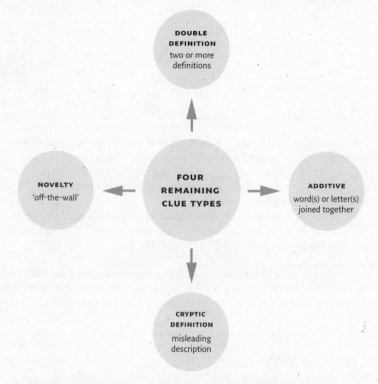

How do we recognize these when no indicator is included?

Punctuation may occasionally be helpful but it's mainly intelligent guesswork that's needed. Are these types therefore harder? You can judge for yourself but I'd say not necessarily.

## 9. The double definition clue

This is simply two, or occasionally more, definitions of the solution side by side. There may be a linking word such as *is* or *'s*, but most frequently there is none, as in this clue.

**DOUBLE DEFINITION CLUE: Polish fan (4)**

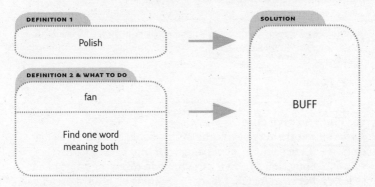

**DOUBLE DEFINITION CLUE: Eggs on toast (6)**

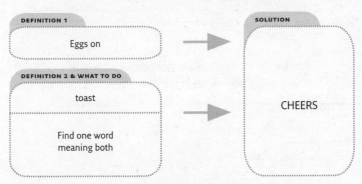

### Indicators for double definition clues:

To repeat, though no specific indicator is given the clue type can often be guessed by its shortness. With only two or three words in a clue, there's a good chance it's a **double definition**. One way of spotting this type of clue is an *and* in a short clue, as in our next example.

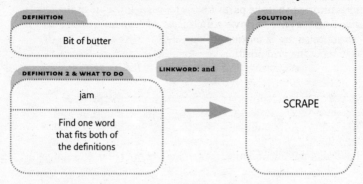

**DEFINITION**

Bit of butter

**DEFINITION 2 & WHAT TO DO**

jam

Find one word
that fits both of
the definitions

**LINKWORD: and**

**SOLUTION**

SCRAPE

## 10. The additive clue

As we saw at the very beginning of this book, an **additive** clue consists of the solution word being split into parts to form the solution. Sometimes known as a **charade** (from the game of charades, rather than its more modern meaning of 'absurd pretence'), it may be helpful to describe it as a simple algebraic expression A + B = solution C. Here is one with several misleading aspects. Note the use of the linking phrase *employed ahead of*, telling you to join part A to part B:

**ADDITIVE CLUE: Pole employed ahead of
young local worker (8)**

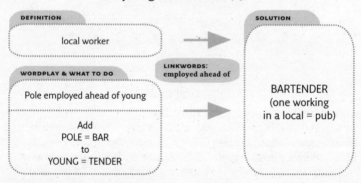

**DEFINITION**

local worker

**WORDPLAY & WHAT TO DO**

Pole employed ahead of young

Add
POLE = BAR
to
YOUNG = TENDER

**LINKWORDS:
employed ahead of**

**SOLUTION**

BARTENDER
(one working
in a local = pub)

### Indicators for additive clues:

With no specific indicator, it's a question rather of spotting that A + B can give C, the solution. Sometimes, as in above example, this is made easier by linkwords such as *facing, alongside, with, next to*, indicating that the parts A and B have to be set alongside each other. In the case of **down** clues, the corresponding linkwords would be *on top of, looking down on* and similar expressions, thereby reflecting the grid position of letters to be entered.

## 11. The cryptic definition clue

There are no component parts at all to this clue, which consists simply of a misleading, usually one-dimensional, way to describe the solution. Depending on how much information is imparted by the clue, it can be very easy or very tough. The best of these clues have an amusing or whimsical air, as in both these examples:

**CRYPTIC DEFINITION CLUE:**
### Work at home temporarily? (7,4)

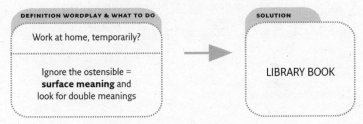

DEFINITION WORDPLAY & WHAT TO DO

Work at home, temporarily?

Ignore the ostensible = **surface meaning** and look for double meanings

SOLUTION

LIBRARY BOOK

**CRYPTIC DEFINITION CLUE:**
### In which all but one in party lose their seats (7,6)

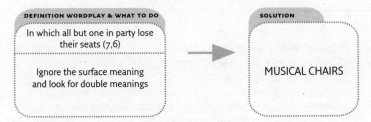

DEFINITION WORDPLAY & WHAT TO DO

In which all but one in party lose their seats (7,6)

Ignore the surface meaning and look for double meanings

SOLUTION

MUSICAL CHAIRS

## Indicators for cryptic definitions:

The nature of this clue type is such that no indicator is ever given. It can be identified either from the fact that nothing in the clue looks like an indicator, and/or from the presence of a question mark. A tip is to look hard at words which have more than one meaning and then think below the surface. Otherwise, wait until some intersecting letters are available.

## 12. The novelty clue

From the inception of crypticity in crosswords, there have been innovative clues conforming to no single pattern which defy categorization into any of the preceding groups. These clues are often solved with extra pleasure.

The setter has found it possible to exploit coincidences or special features of a word. As with the cryptic definition type, the solver is asked to think laterally and throw away any misleading images created by the clue. In some rare circumstances when an especially novel idea is used, there may not even be a proper definition. There are more examples of the **novelty** clue in Chapter 8 but, as a taster, here is one:

**NOVELTY CLUE:**
**Eccentric as three-quarters of the characters in Fiji? (5)**

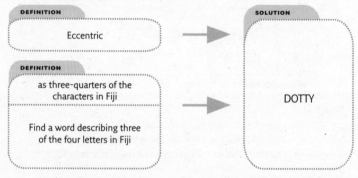

| DEFINITION | | SOLUTION |
| --- | --- | --- |
| Eccentric | → | |
| DEFINITION | | |
| as three-quarters of the characters in Fiji | → | DOTTY |
| Find a word describing three of the four letters in Fiji | | |

---

**TOP TIP – CLUE FREQUENCY**

Given the twelve clue types identified, which are the most commonly found? The answer to this is that frequency patterns vary according to setter and newspaper but that the **additive**, **anagram**, **cryptic definition** and **sandwich** types are the most common; they may indeed account for more than half the clues in many crosswords. It may help you to know that there are rarely more than two or three of the following types in any one puzzle: **hidden**, **homophone**, **all-in-one**, **novelty**, **letter switch**.

# Letter selection indicators

Before moving on to solving clues, we have to consider how individual letters within clues are signposted. We have seen what sort of indicators go with what sort of clues; now we'll take a look at another commonly used indicator which is essential to solving skills. Take this clue as an example:

ADDITIVE CLUE: **Lettuce constituent of salad, primarily (3)**

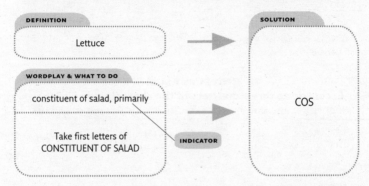

Experienced solvers would be immediately drawn towards the word *primarily* as it indicates that the first letter or (as in this case) letters of the preceding words are to be selected as building blocks to the solution. In more complex clues they could then be subject to further treatment, such as forming part of an anagram, but here they are used simply to form *cos*, the *lettuce* salad ingredient.

There are many alternative ways of showing that the first letter is to be manipulated in some way. Some of these indicators are: *starter, lead, source, opening, top, introduction* and so on. They may be extended to the plural form too with the use of, say, *beginnings, foremost* and *heads*. Note that *bit of, part of* and suchlike by long-standing convention always indicate the first letter.

Other positions within words are indicated in a similar fashion. The last letter can be *end, back, finally, tail* and the middle letter *centre, heart,* and all of the inside letters of a word can be *innards, contents, stuffing*.

In their negative **takeaway** guise, they can be *headless, unopened, failing to start*; and *empty* signifies that the whole of the innards of a word is to be removed.

Overleaf are some examples of letter selection indicators at work:

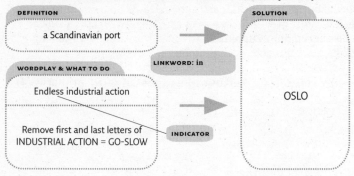

**TAKEAWAY CLUE:**
**Endless industrial action in a Scandinavian port (4)**

DEFINITION

a Scandinavian port

LINKWORD: in

WORDPLAY & WHAT TO DO

Endless industrial action

Remove first and last letters of
INDUSTRIAL ACTION = GO-SLOW

INDICATOR

SOLUTION

OSLO

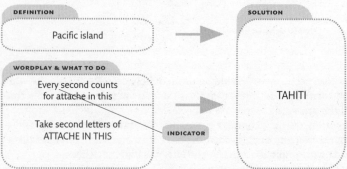

**ADDITIVE CLUE:**
**Every second counts for attaché in this Pacific island (6)**

DEFINITION

Pacific island

WORDPLAY & WHAT TO DO

Every second counts
for attache in this

Take second letters of
ATTACHE IN THIS

INDICATOR

SOLUTION

TAHITI

After a time, you will become familiar with looking beyond and through
the surface meaning of a word doing duty as an indicator so that you
realise what you are required to do to the relevant letter(s) or word(s).

---

**TOP TIP – LETTER SELECTION INDICATORS**
Beware **letter selection** indicators that, depending on the setter's policy, can do double or triple duty:

*Endless*: take away last letter only, or first and last letters.

*Head*: first letter, or take away first letter (in its sense of *behead*).

*Cut*: last letter takeaway, sandwich (inside type), anagram (in its
slang sense of *drunk*).

*Back*: last letter, reversal.

Note that in the example below *extremely* indicates first and last letters; in some crosswords it can indicate the last letter only of the preceding word.

**ADDITIVE CLUE: Robin's slayer gets extremely sharp weapon (7)**

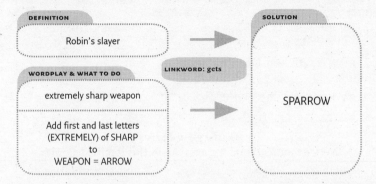

DEFINITION

Robin's slayer

WORDPLAY & WHAT TO DO

LINKWORD: gets

extremely sharp weapon

Add first and last letters
(EXTREMELY) of SHARP
to
WEAPON = ARROW

SOLUTION

SPARROW

There are examples of indicators throughout this book but it would take an impossibly large volume to include all those used. There are books which list more (as covered in Chapter 12) but even they are not comprehensive. The point to bear in mind is that once you are aware of the possible clue types, you will often be able to infer from a word or words what you are being instructed to do.

What can be difficult, however, is where the same common word in the English language serves as an indicator for several clue types. The words *in* and *about* are the most problematic examples of this and you will find more about these and equally troublesome words in Chapter 10.

## Chapters 1–3: summary

Here are two charts offering in summary form the basic points of Chapters 1, 2 and 3. First, a summary of clue types, typical indicators and what the solver must do:

| CLUE TYPE | TYPICAL INDICATORS | WHAT TO DO |
|---|---|---|
| **Types 1–8** | **Indicators included in clue** | |
| ANAGRAM | New, mixed, changing, drunk, in error | Change letters to another word |
| SANDWICH (OUTSIDE) | Holding, keeps, contains | Put some letters outside others |
| SANDWICH (INSIDE) | In, breaks, cutting, interrupts | Put some letters inside others |
| HOMOPHONE | Mentioned, we hear | Find a word sounding like another |
| HIDDEN | Some, partly, within | Find a word within other words |
| REVERSAL (ACROSS CLUE) | Back, over, returns | Turn letters backwards |
| REVERSAL (DOWN CLUE) | Up, over, served up | Turn letters upwards |
| TAKEAWAY | Less, without, drop, cast | Deduct some letter(s) from a word |
| LETTER SWITCH | For, replacing, moving | Exchange or move letters |
| ALL-IN-ONE | Various, depending on wordplay | Use wordplay to find solution which is then defined by the wordplay |
| **Types 9–12** | **Indicators (usually) not included in clue** | |
| ADDITIVE | Usually none given | Add letter(s) to other letter(s) |
| DOUBLE DEFINITION | None given | Find solution from two or more distinct definitions, side by side |
| CRYPTIC DEFINITION | None given | Find solution from puns, hints, ambiguities; ignore surface reading |
| NOVELTY | None given | Think laterally |

Second, here's how each clue type can be used for the same solution word *time*, (defined as the US magazine in 10 clues). Indicators are underlined.

| CLUE TYPE | CLUES | WHAT TO DO |
|---|---|---|
| **Types 1–8** | | |
| ANAGRAM | <u>New</u> item in magazine | Change letters of ITEM |
| SANDWICH (OUTSIDE) | Match <u>bringing in</u> millions for magazine | Put MATCH = TIE outside MILLIONS = M |
| SANDWICH (INSIDE) | Millions <u>put into</u> match magazine | Put MILLIONS = M inside MATCH = TIE |
| HOMOPHONE | Herb <u>mentioned</u> in magazine | Find a word for a HERB sounding like TIME (THYME) |
| HIDDEN | <u>Some</u> sentimental magazine | Find a word within SENTIMENTAL |
| REVERSAL (ACROSS CLUE) | Magazine issue <u>backed</u> | Reverse ISSUE = EMIT |
| REVERSAL (DOWN CLUE) | Magazine issue <u>taken up</u> | Reverse ISSUE = EMIT |
| TAKEAWAY | <u>Nameless</u> chaps behind note in magazine | Remove NAME = N from MEN; add NOTE = TI |
| LETTER SWITCH | Magazine volume, one <u>for</u> nothing | Replace NOTHING = O in VOLUME = TOME with I |
| ALL-IN-ONE | Male, <u>interned</u> in Windsor is doing this? | Put MALE = M inside WINDSOR = TIE |
| **Types 9–12** | | |
| ADDITIVE | Note yours truly in magazine | Add NOTE = TI to YOURS TRULY = ME |
| DOUBLE DEFINITION | Bird magazine | Two ways of expressing time, BIRD is time in prison |
| CRYPTIC DEFINITION | Wilde did it in a sentence | Think of Oscar W in prison |
| NOVELTY | Spell centimetre: this is <u>in</u> middle – <u>in</u> middle! | Find TIME centrally inside CENTRE |

## WHY ARE SOME CLUES MORE DIFFICULT THAN OTHERS?

Levels of cryptic difficulty are shown by these **sandwich** clues, all using the same definition *don't worry* and all giving the same answer but with differing wordplay:

- Ned catches vermin, don't worry (5,4): The letters to be manipulated are in the clue ie *Ned* outside *vermin*
- Edward catches vermin, don't worry (5,4): A small change from *Edward* to *Ned* is required
- Boy catches mice, don't worry (5,4): Two changes are needed as *mice* has to become *vermin*

I hope you got *never mind* as the answer in each case. If you didn't, never mind, as the point remains that while clue structures are the same, synonyms have to be found before the sandwich can be made and it is this that makes solving more difficult. Of course, unusual words as answers and obscure references are other causes of difficulty.

# 4: Tips for Solving Clues

*"This isn't biography. It's the only thing the English are good at...*
*crossword puzzles."*
Alan Bennett, *Kafka's Dick*

Having considered clue types and various points associated with each,
we will now consider some tips on how you might go about solving them.

Seasoned solvers have many ways of uncovering a clue's solution. The ones following are in no particular recommended order of
importance, except that the first two are often quoted as ways to get
started.

## 1. Find the definition
As you know by now, the definition part of nearly all clues is either
at the beginning or end of a clue. Identifying it quickly, and assess-
ing the definition in conjunction with word-length shown, allows
the possibility of a good initial guess which can then be checked
against wordplay before entry.

## 2. Find an indicator and/or clue type
Not all clues have indicators, as we have seen, but where they do,
try to use them to identify the clue type. For example, you may spot
a familiar anagram indicator such as *mixed* or *battered* and thence
compare the letters in the **anagram fodder** with the word-length
of the solution given. If they correspond, there is a good chance
that you have identified the wordplay element of the clue and can
develop that into a possible solution.

## 3. Ignore the scenario
Setters do their best to produce clues which paint a smooth, realis-
tic picture, referred to as the *surface meaning* or just *surface*. Try to
ignore it however and look at the individual components in front of
you. Take the clue overleaf, seemingly about a party:

**ADDITIVE CLUE: Last ones in get no sherry trifle (3)**

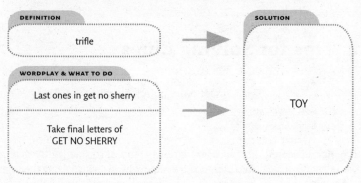

| DEFINITION | SOLUTION |
|---|---|
| trifle | |
| **WORDPLAY & WHAT TO DO** | TOY |
| Last ones in get no sherry | |
| Take final letters of GET NO SHERRY | |

You can be pretty sure that recalling memories of children's parties will not be productive. It's just a clever deception by the use of *ones* for *letters* and a **letter selection** indicator, *last* (see Chapter 3, page 31), leading to *trifle = toy*.

> **TOP TIP – SURFACE MEANING**
> The ability to look beyond surface meaning is what newbies find the hardest part of cracking a cryptic clue. My advice can only be to keep trying.

## 4. Exploit word-lengths
Use friendly word-lengths such as 4,2,3,4 with the central two being perhaps something like *in the* or *of the*; and 4,4,1,4 nearly always embracing the letter A, from which something like *once upon a time* may be the guessable answer.

## 5. Study every word
Consider each word carefully, separately and together. Disregard phrases which go naturally together such as, say, *silver wedding*, and split them into their parts. It could be that the definition is *silver* on its own and *wedding* is part of the wordplay.

In doing this, think of all the meanings of a word rather than the one that comes first into your head.

For example, forget *drink* in its marine sense in the next clue and switch to *alcohol*. The indicator *some* makes it a **hidden clue**.

## HIDDEN CLUE: **Some termed ocean the drink (5)**

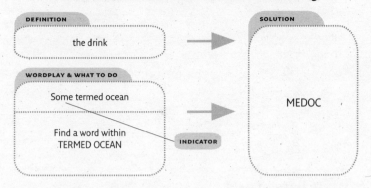

Here is another misleading image in the second example below, which has nothing to do with music:

## HOMOPHONE CLUE: **Cor Anglais's third piece heard (3)**

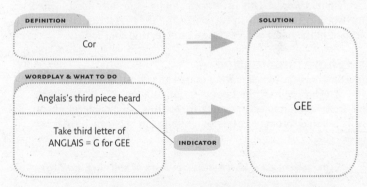

Last, an instance, overleaf, of how separating the sentence into even its smallest parts is sometimes needed. This clue is a further demonstration of a **letter selection** indicator, *empty* for *lane* leaving the two letters *le*, and of a deceptive definition.

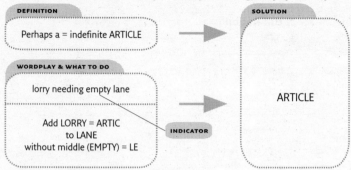

DEFINITION

Perhaps a = indefinite ARTICLE

SOLUTION

WORDPLAY & WHAT TO DO

lorry needing empty lane

Add LORRY = ARTIC
to LANE
without middle (EMPTY) = LE

INDICATOR

ARTICLE

## 6. Write bars in grid

Given word-lengths that indicate more than one complete word (e.g. 3-7, or 3,7), some solvers automatically write the word divisions as bar-lines into the grid and find that helps. The bars can be either vertical or horizontal depending on whether they are split words or hyphenated words. This little trick can be especially useful when the word to be found is in two parts and the first letter, say, of the second of the parts is given by an intersecting solution.

## 7. Ignore punctuation

In a nutshell, only exclamation marks and question marks at the end of a clue are meaningful; other punctuation should usually be ignored. For example, the **anagram fodder** can include letters or words with a comma or other punctuation in between, as in this tricky clue:

**ALL-IN-ONE ANAGRAM CLUE: Sort of roll, A-E etc? (9)**

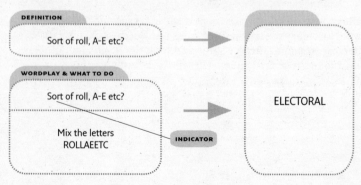

DEFINITION

Sort of roll, A-E etc?

WORDPLAY & WHAT TO DO

Sort of roll, A-E etc?

Mix the letters
ROLLAEETC

INDICATOR

ELECTORAL

Another example of this is seen in the clue that follows:

**HIDDEN CLUE: Rabbit produced from magic hat? Terrific (7)**

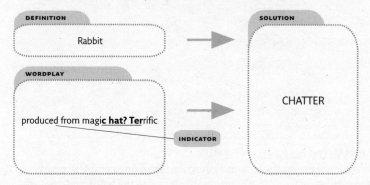

The question mark and capital T are both to be ignored. There is more on misleading punctuation in Chapter 9, pages 88-92.

## 8. Guess

An inspired guess can work wonders; you just feel that you know the answer without recognizing why. I have watched this intuitive process in my workshops and it's magical. On one occasion a lady in her late 80s, a solver evidently for almost as long, was often able to come up with the answers before anyone else but had no idea how she had done so. Unfortunately, this method doesn't work for everybody.

## 9. Think comma

One of the most useful tips I received as a novice was to imagine a comma in any part of the clue sentence. As we have seen in nearly all the examples so far, clues consist frequently of a string of words, each one of which has a part to play, and separating them into their meaningful parts can prove very helpful. In the next clue, imagining a pause between the last two words makes the solution much easier.

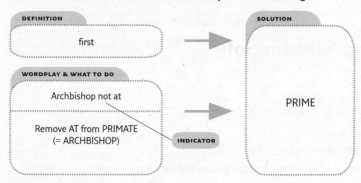

**TAKEAWAY CLUE: Archbishop? Not at first (5)**

DEFINITION

first

WORDPLAY & WHAT TO DO

Archbishop not at

Remove AT from PRIMATE
(= ARCHBISHOP)

INDICATOR

SOLUTION

PRIME

## 10. Try to memorise frequently-occurring small words

The same three- and four-letter words inevitably crop up a lot and successful solvers store up words like *pig*, *sow*, *cow*, *tup* and *hog* for *farm animal* (or even just *animal*) and smartly bring these into their deliberations. I realise that many of my readers will have better things to remember, so let's move on.

## 11. Advice on cracking anagrams

After you have identified an **anagram** indicator, counted the number of letters in the **anagram fodder**, including any abbreviations, and seen that they make up the given word-length, what techniques are there to find the solution?

People have their own familiar way of sorting out anagrams. Some find using Scrabble tiles works well; often the simplest method involves finding the right combination from careful scrutiny of the letters, looking for the commonly occurring *-ing*, *-tion*, *-er*, *-or* endings.

If this does not work, the anagram fodder can then be written down in various ways: in a straight line, in a diamond shape, in a circle, in reverse order or in random order. With longer anagrams, this can involve several rewrites in different orders until the answer emerges. In cases where the definition is something not very specific, such as *plant* or *animal*, it may be best to defer resolution until some intersecting letters have been entered.

Finally there are electronic aids as listed in Chapter 12 which can take all the pain (but maybe some of the enjoyment) out of the process.

# 5: Tips for Solving the Whole Puzzle

*"They say children in kindergarten must play in order to learn. What do they mean, children? Crossword puzzles learned grown folks more words than school teachers."*
Will Rogers

Now let's consider some points for tackling the whole of a puzzle.

## 1. Write in pencil or ink?
I'm not sure it matters much as long as you avoid inking in firmly before you have worked out both the definition and wordplay. There is nothing worse than being held up for a long time by an incorrect entry made in haste. A thoughtful Christmas present bought for me some years ago was the delightful compromise of a pen with ink that could be erased.

## 2. Empty grid: how to start?
You have a puzzle in front of you which looks totally impossible – maybe you start to feel inadequate but remember that most puzzles, by accident or design, give you at least one clue to get you going and all you have to do is find it! It may be a **hidden** clue; after all, the letters of the solution are there facing you as part of the clue. So scan the clues for a **hidden** indicator. But supposing the mean setter this time gives you no **hidden** clues. What should you do when there appears to be no way in? There are various points:

- It is rare for there to be no **anagram** clue, so why not scan for an **anagram** indicator? Do inspect the longest words as they are more likely to be clued by anagrams than shorter ones. Once found, the letters are there as with **hidden** clues, waiting to be unscrambled.
- Try to spot an obvious definition. One experienced solver told me he can see a definition nearly always instantly – but that was after 40 years of solving!
- At this stage it's a good idea to find a clue that seems to be within your areas of interests or expertise. For example, in

my case it is always comforting for me to spot clues which seem to have a musical, political, food or sporting component. Of course I have to be aware that I may be being led up the garden path.

- Look for short solutions of three letters because there are fewer words that can fit the space indicated. While it's rewarding to get the 15-letter word at 1 across immediately, that is rare.
- Try the compound phrases that are present in most puzzles. As covered earlier, the likes of 3,2,4 and 4,4,1,4 are a gift in the sense that the shorter lengths can often be guessed.
- Keep in mind that the tense of the clue and the solution must be the same. So look for plurals, -*ing* and -*ed* in potential definitions. Try to formulate an answer from this but beware inking in such endings in error.
- Try to find proper names and ask yourself why they may have been included. Getting into the setter's mind in this respect and in other aspects of cryptic clues can be rewarding.

---

**TOP TIP – WHERE TO START?**

More than one solver I know considers that you should look at the bottom right hand corner first as the setter, having written the clues in order from 1 across, is tired by the time the bottom of the grid is reached. Hence the clues are easier than elsewhere. Based on my own setting process, I'm sceptical about this but, nonetheless, if that approach helps you to gain the confidence essential to solving, I'd say stick with it, though it's harder to complete a puzzle after starting at the bottom!

## 3. How to continue?

After one clue is solved, where next? Try building on the most promising (i.e. less common) of the intersecting letters you have available. Don't attempt clues for which you have no letters until you become convinced you can make no progress with the letters you have. Crossword solving is a process of gains being built up cumulatively and, at this early stage, there may or may not be gains to make.

Try a little harder to crack clues that yield the best follow-on letters, e.g. those running across the top and down the sides. As one of my correspondents put it, first letters are usually worth a lot. Also when more letters are available, you may find that you can anticipate solutions from letter patterns such as -*ation*, -*ive*, -*ally* and the like.

## ARE SOME GRIDS EASIER THAN OTHERS?

Those in which the highest number of initial letters of answers are potentially available to help with other answers are likely to prove best for new solvers. This is shown in these two below, the bottom one in principle being an easier solve.

# 6. The Knowledge

*"Crosswords are notoriously worked at by quite humble members of society."*
*Times* Leader 1928, referring to the USA

Some items which are common to many puzzles and which, after a time, you will take for granted are covered in this next chapter. Just as it takes London cabbies some years to acquire all the information needed for their task, so it is with crosswords. What follows is a randomly ordered set of items that I hope helps you along the way to becoming a solver of excellence.

## 1. Numerals
Numerals, chiefly roman, are common so in alphabetical order you will find:

| | | | |
|---|---|---|---|
| eleven | xi | hundred | c |
| fifty | l | hundred and fifty | cl |
| fifty-one | li | nine | ix |
| five | v | six | vi |
| five hundred | d | ten | x |
| four | iv | thousand | m and k |

Numbers such as eighteen (XVIII) are unlikely to be met for obvious reasons.

## 2. Compass points
Equally common are compass points. The abbreviations for north, south, east and west and their two-letter combinations need no listing here but look for *point* or *quarter* which can do duty for any of the four. This can involve testing each in turn to see whether it

yields part of, or the full, solution. Very occasionally you may need to think of three-letter compass points, as in this clue:

**SANDWICH CLUE: Wind bearing round spit (7)**

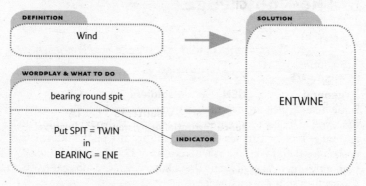

DEFINITION
Wind

SOLUTION
ENTWINE

WORDPLAY & WHAT TO DO
bearing round spit

Put SPIT = TWIN
in
BEARING = ENE

INDICATOR

N,E,W and S are Bridge players too (see 13 below).

## 3. Foreign languages

Some knowledge of foreign languages is needed but only of simple words in the more familiar, usually European, languages. Thus German articles *der*, *die* or *das*; French ones *le*, *la* or *les*; and Spanish *el*, *la* or *los*; and the equivalent indefinite articles in these languages are regarded as fair game, as are common French words such as *oui*, *rue* and *et*. Look out for misleading indications of Frenchness such as *Nice*, *Angers* and *Nancy*. Here's a more straightforward example:

**ADDITIVE CLUE: Misery of the French couple (7)**

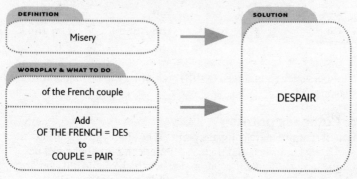

DEFINITION
Misery

SOLUTION
DESPAIR

WORDPLAY & WHAT TO DO
of the French couple

Add
OF THE FRENCH = DES
to
COUPLE = PAIR

## 4. Military types

Military types can appear in their abbreviated form as below but also more generally as soldier(s), officer(s), rank, unit(s) and the like.

| | | | |
|---|---|---|---|
| American soldier | GI | gunners | RA |
| artillery | RA | lieutenant | LT |
| colonel | COL | officer | NCO, OC |
| engineers | RE | other ranks | OR |
| general | GEN | soldiers | OR |
| | | volunteers | TA* |

**\*once Territorial Army, now Army Reserve**

## 5. Rivers

Rivers feature in crosswords as the abbreviation *R* and also, because of their size, the *Po*, *Exe* or *Dee*. As always it's trial and error that unlocks which particular one is required. Another more esoteric expression of *river* is *flower* (see Chapter 10, page 102).

## 6. Alphabets

A brief recall of some alphabets may come in handy. In particular:

**GREEK LETTERS**

| | | | |
|---|---|---|---|
| beta | chi | delta | eta |
| iota | mu | nu | phi |
| pi | psi | rho | tau |
| xi | | | |

**NATO**

| | | | |
|---|---|---|---|
| alpha | bravo | Charlie | delta |
| echo | foxtrot | golf | hotel |
| India | Juliet | kilo | lima |
| Mike | November | Oscar | papa |
| Quebec | Romeo | sierra | tango |
| uniform | victor | whiskey | X-ray |
| Yankee | Zulu | | |

## 7. Cricket terms

Though many sports and games do appear in crosswords (golf and tennis perhaps more than soccer or rugby), the quaint often short terms and frequent abbreviations used in cricket are a gift to setters. Non-cricket loving participants on my workshops tell me this is a cause of frustration, so here are the cricket abbreviations likely to be encountered:

| | | | |
|---|---|---|---|
| bowled | B | maiden | M |
| bye | B | one-day international | ODI |
| caught | C or CT | over | O |
| duck | O | run or runs | R |
| eleven, side | XI | run out | RO |
| fifty | L | stumped | ST |
| hundred | C | wicket | W |
| length | L | wide | W |

In addition, these cricket terms are common: batting (IN), cricket side (LEG and ON), extra (BYE), ton (C = one hundred) and deliveries (OVER).

## 8. Chemical elements

Remember your chemical elements? Here are those most beloved of setters:

| | | | |
|---|---|---|---|
| arsenic | AS | calcium | CA |
| copper | CU | gold | AU |
| helium | HE | hydrogen | H |
| iron | FE | lead | PB |
| nitrogen | N | potassium | K |
| silver | AG | tin | SN |
| tungsten | W | | |

The following wonderfully misleading effort uses one of these:

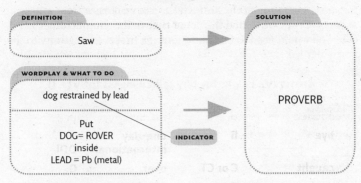

**SANDWICH CLUE: Saw dog restrained by lead (7)**

DEFINITION
Saw

SOLUTION
PROVERB

WORDPLAY & WHAT TO DO
dog restrained by lead

INDICATOR

Put
DOG= ROVER
inside
LEAD = Pb (metal)

## 9. The City of London

Though now effectively split across several postal areas including Canary Wharf, in crosswords it is still thought of as the old Square Mile; actually not even all of it (EC2), just EC for City or The City in wordplay, as below in a clue with a debatable sentiment:

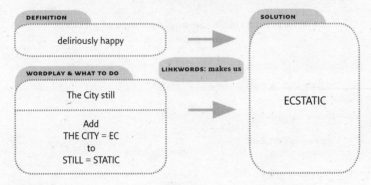

**ADDITIVE CLUE: The City still makes us deliriously happy (8)**

DEFINITION
deliriously happy

SOLUTION
ECSTATIC

LINKWORDS: makes us

WORDPLAY & WHAT TO DO
The City still

Add
THE CITY = EC
to
STILL = STATIC

## 10. Chess

Chess notations that appear are: bishop (B), king (K), knight (N), pawn (P), queen (Q), rook (R). In addition, the word *board* in a clue may well be referring to chess.

## 11. Names

In part of the wordplay, names of boys and girls, arguably unfairly, can be indicated by the terse *boy* or *girl*, etc. Probably *Ed*, *Ted*, *Di* and *Ian* (the latter surprisingly reckoned often to be a Scotsman) are the most common but the best advice is to work back from other aspects of the clue to find the name in question. In this rather hard clue, you would need to find the definition first before coming to the particular lad:

**ADDITIVE CLUE: Toy boy talked incessantly (7,2)**

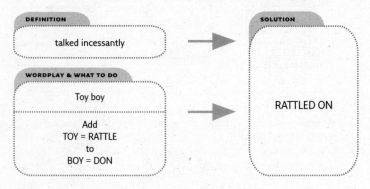

DEFINITION

talked incessantly

WORDPLAY & WHAT TO DO

Toy boy

Add
TOY = RATTLE
to
BOY = DON

SOLUTION

RATTLED ON

... and here's a less common name in an enjoyable clue:

**SANDWICH CLUE: Wide-angle picture of girl kept by her parents (8)**

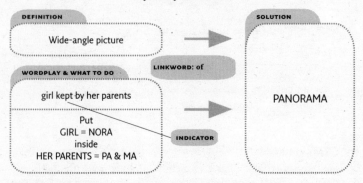

DEFINITION

Wide-angle picture

LINKWORD: of

WORDPLAY & WHAT TO DO

girl kept by her parents

Put
GIRL = NORA
inside
HER PARENTS = PA & MA

INDICATOR

SOLUTION

PANORAMA

## 12. Setters

Despite the fact that many newspapers do not reveal the names of their setters, he or she does appear in clues. This can be as *Yours Truly*, *I* or *me* within wordplay. Here's an example from a newspaper that names its setters:

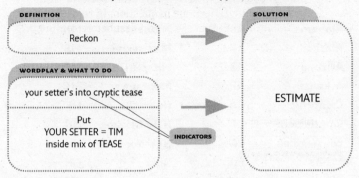

**SANDWICH INCLUDING ANAGRAM CLUE:**
**Reckon your setter's into cryptic tease (8)**

DEFINITION

Reckon

WORDPLAY & WHAT TO DO

your setter's into cryptic tease

Put
YOUR SETTER = TIM
inside mix of TEASE

INDICATORS

SOLUTION

ESTIMATE

## 13. Bridge

Bridge notation features in terms of north, south, east and west in abbreviated form and this can extend to Bridge partners as here:

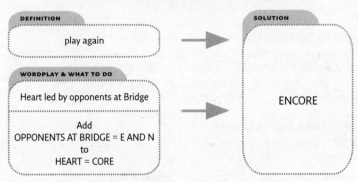

**ADDITIVE CLUE:**
**Heart led by opponents at bridge – play again! (6)**

DEFINITION

play again

WORDPLAY & WHAT TO DO

Heart led by opponents at Bridge

Add
OPPONENTS AT BRIDGE = E AND N
to
HEART = CORE

SOLUTION

ENCORE

Sometimes in harder cryptics, the single word "partners" is meant to be taken as being bridge partners N & S or E & W.

## 14. Accents and other punctuation

Accents, hyphens and apostrophes are of course included in clue sentences but, by convention, they are not entered into the grid. For example, *its* and *it's* in clues would be entered in the same way (as *its*) in the grid.

## 15. Some US states and cities

Those states which appear more than others are in the box below:

| | | | |
|---|---|---|---|
| Alabama | AL | Minnesota | MN |
| Alaska | AK | Mississippi | MS |
| Arizona | AZ | Missouri | MO |
| Arkansas | AR | Montana | MT |
| California | CA | Nebraska | NE |
| Connecticut | CT | New Orleans | NO |
| Los Angeles | LA | New York | NY |
| Maine | ME | Ohio | OH |
| Maryland | MD | Oklahoma | OK |
| Massachusetts | MA | Oregon | OR |
| Michigan | MI | Washington | WA |

## 16. Workers

The word *worker* could be a reference to the human kind but, more likely, it will be a synonym for *ant* or *bee*.

## 17. On board

Phrases such as *on board* can be related to chess, e.g. men or pieces, or ships. In addition, SS (= steam ship) can be exploited in wording such as *on board* in a **sandwich** clue. Thus a word like *train* may be inserted between *s* and *s* to give *strains*.

## 18. Some Latin terms

These are perhaps the most common:

| | | | |
|---|---|---|---|
| and so on | ETC | present day | AD |
| afternoon | PM | see | V |
| approximately, about | CA | that is or that's | IE |
| morning | AM | thus | SIC |

# 7. Ten Things to Consider When Stuck

> *"Congratulations to all who completed this puzzle which was printed with the wrong grid."*
> Sunday Telegraph

Even the best solvers get held up or seriously stuck at times. Here are ten reasons why you may also hit a wall, with suggestions as to how to make a breakthrough.

## 1. Check for a wrong entry

The first point to consider is whether you have made a mistake in an earlier entry. Once a word is 'inked' into the grid, you naturally become reluctant to consider other possibilities for the solution in question.

Even experienced hands like me trip up by inserting incorrect answers into the grid too quickly, for example without having matched wordplay to definition or vice versa. It's maddening to spend a long time working from wrong assumptions so do check this possibility first.

## 2. Ignore the surface reading

The vital fact to keep in mind is that the setter's aim is to produce a sentence that appears to mean one thing but may well, and usu-ally does, mean something totally different. In the very best clues, this is achieved by the creation of a highly misleading image. The solver's response is to enjoy the image but ignore it – the solution may come out after a close examination of each word rather than appreciation of the scenario presented. Try not to miss the subtlety of a clue, but only after being sure of the solution.

## 3. Look carefully again and consider each word in the clue

Cunning setters find ways of using familiar combinations and juxtapositions which require splitting before any progress can be made. Consider the clue below. You may well have got stuck on this until you realised that the two words *British Isles* have to be separated to uncover the definition.

SANDWICH CLUE: **Ambassador travels round British Isles (8)**

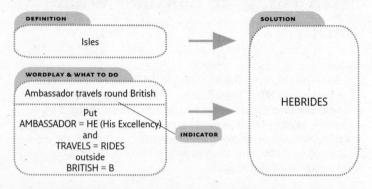

DEFINITION

Isles

SOLUTION

WORDPLAY & WHAT TO DO

Ambassador travels round British

Put
AMBASSADOR = HE (His Excellency)
and
TRAVELS = RIDES
outside
BRITISH = B

INDICATOR

HEBRIDES

---

**TOP TIP – PARTS OF SPEECH**
Use of misleading parts of speech is a strong feature. Participants in my workshops are misled time and again by this and my suggestion is that, when temporarily stuck, you reconsider carefully every word of the clue which could have an alternative part of speech.

## 4. Endings
Based on a definition in the past tense, you may have pencilled or, even worse, inked in the ending *-ed* when the actual solution is, say, *caught* or *known*. Similar problems can arise after putting in an *-s* or an *-ing* – sensible practice, usually, but needing reconsideration when you are stuck.

## 5. Take a break to do something else
This is the most popular tip of all from solvers. Doing the washing up or taking the dog for a walk has the most liberating effect on the blocked crossword mind. You may find that this extends to getting a solution the next morning – or even during the night.

## 6. Ring the help line
If you cannot wait that long, the solution to the current day's puzzle can be obtained via a paid phone call to the number shown at the foot of each day's puzzle.

## 7. 'Cheat' via electronic aids and the internet

Crosswords are rarely a competition so you make your own rules as regards using electronic aids. Using dictionaries to confirm a solution is just common sense; going further to root out a solution electronically is now much easier than hitherto as word completion tools, especially prevalent now on the internet, virtually guarantee finding tricky answers.

But is this cheating? Typically half of my students will be firmly against what they see as cheating; the other half see it differently as a means of shortening a process which would anyway have led to the answer later. The ultimate, if that's what you want, is a programme called Crossword Maestro. It reckons to solve a high percentage of clues but that surely takes the fun out of the whole thing. Incidentally, the developer claims his programme knows over 4000 anagram indicators. Without going that far, and if conventional dictionary/thesaurus hunting has failed or is too time-consuming, you can try a word completion tool. Some of these are listed in Chapter 12.

You can also seek help with a particular clue via a website such as www.answerbank.com. This, I'm told, nearly always finds someone kind enough to give an answer. Finally you can type a clue into Google and see what comes up. Impressively, on a random test, this threw up the answer to six of seven clues from different newspapers!

## 8. Consult the blog

See Chapter 12. Not only does this usually give the answer on the day of the publication but it helpfully gives the wordplay or an explanation.

## 9. Phone a friend

It's remarkable how two or more brains working on a clue can come up with answers much more effectively than one.

## 10. Ask Alexa and her like

One assumes that artificial intelligence (AI) will before very long facilitate the solving of all crossword clues, perhaps even setting crosswords too!

## ROBOTS TO KILL OFF CROSSWORD COMPILERS INSIDE 15 YEARS

This *Daily Mirror* 2018 headline looked more suitable for a 1st April story than 27th February when it actually appeared.

# PART 2

# MASTERING THE FINER POINTS

## 8. Finer Points: by Clue Type

> *"The nicest thing about a crossword is that you know there's a solution. A crossword is an unusual puzzle in that you can derive enjoyment from it, even if you cannot complete it entirely (provided that the setter has shown wit, wisdom and elegance)."*
>
> Stephen Sondheim, who introduced Americans to the cryptic crossword puzzle, *Secrets of the Setters*

We move up from basics to consider the finer points of clues and puzzles. The charts from now on have wordplay analysis as an explanation rather than an indication of what to do.

Assuming that you wish to go along with the optimism of the above quotation, let's start with the finer points associated with clue types, and then those that apply generally to all clues.

### 1. The anagram clue: finer points

From now on, we will indicate which words form the **anagram fodder** by an asterisk (*).

#### Anagram fodder: which letters? (1)

Some crosswords require you to find an interim solution and then make an anagram of that. Called an **indirect anagram**, the practice is almost extinct, as it should be. However, where there is a unique interim solution such as *omicron* (*pi*'s predecessor in the Greek alphabet), you may see a clue such as the one overleaf.

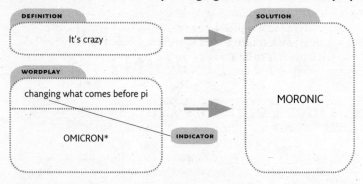

### TOP TIP – ANAGRAM FREQUENCY

It is rare for there to be no anagrams in a cryptic puzzle and equally rare to find more than about eight in total (depending on the newspaper), with two-part anagrams counting as one whole-word anagram.

## Anagram fodder: which letters? (2)

The anagram fodder can be part of a hyphenated word, as here:

ANAGRAM CLUE: **Aspiring to achieve first in Wimbledon, double-faulted (5-2)**

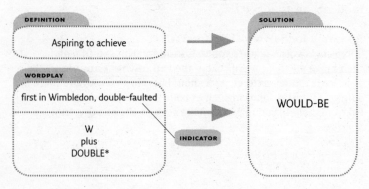

## Position of the indicator

While anagrams are always indicated in one of the many ways already covered in Chapter 3, the position of the indicator is not always immediately next to the **anagram fodder**. In the clue below, a letter has to be deducted before the anagram can be unscrambled:

**ANAGRAM CLUE: Neglectful having left off dicky bow (9)**

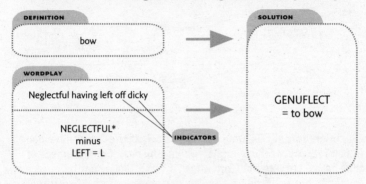

DEFINITION

bow

WORDPLAY

Neglectful having left off dicky

NEGLECTFUL*
minus
LEFT = L

INDICATORS

SOLUTION

GENUFLECT
= to bow

## 2. The sandwich clue: finer points

The basis of this very common clue type, something inside something else, is often the technique that delays solvers, so its tricks and quirks should repay study.

Its use in any one clue may be in conjunction with, say, an **anagram**, and be indicated by a less than obvious indicator. In the following example, the indicator *stop* is used in its sense of *block* or *plug* (perhaps more normally *stop up*):

**SANDWICH CLUE: Nothing stops Chelsea playing tie (8)**

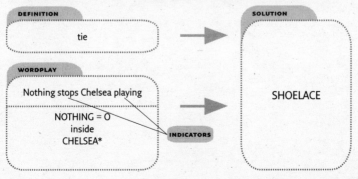

DEFINITION

tie

WORDPLAY

Nothing stops Chelsea playing

NOTHING = O
inside
CHELSEA*

INDICATORS

SOLUTION

SHOELACE

Sometimes the element to be sandwiched is difficult to disentangle, as in this clue:

**SANDWICH CLUE: Rather restricting the setter? I don't care! (8)**

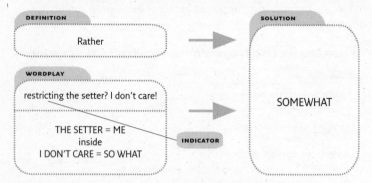

DEFINITION
Rather

SOLUTION

WORDPLAY
restricting the setter? I don't care!

INDICATOR

THE SETTER = ME
inside
I DON'T CARE = SO WHAT

SOMEWHAT

One might initially assume that *I don't care* is the definition when in fact it is part of the wordplay which consists of all the words of the clue except the first word *rather*. As so often, a comma must be imagined between the first and second words before you can solve the clue.

---

**TOP TIP – 'HIDDEN' VS. 'SANDWICH' CLUES**
I find workshop newbies do confuse **hidden** and **sandwich** clues, partly because their indicators are similar. The difference is that in **hidden** clues, the word to be found is contained exactly (albeit with intervening punctuation sometimes) within the clue sentence. In **sandwich** clues, the solution word is to be constructed by the solver from the separate elements available.

The sandwich can be formed with a kind of reverse construction, as here:

### SANDWICH CLUE: **Fall in love? On the contrary, wilt (5)**

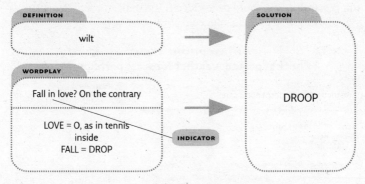

The next example is a most deceptive sandwich in that, signalled by *fences*, the clue is to read as *by* surrounds *alone = separated*:

### SANDWICH CLUE: **Bull is separated from the herd by fences (7)**

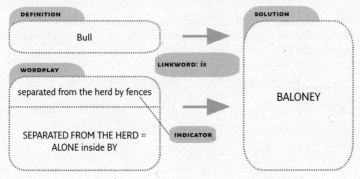

The message is that study of each word individually pays off.

## 3. The homophone clue: finer points

In the best clue-writing, you should be left in no doubt in a **homophone** clue as to which word is the solution and which the wordplay. For example, the solution to the next clue could be *rain* or *rein* and the ambiguity would be avoided if the indicator *reported* were moved to the end of the sentence.

**HOMOPHONE CLUE:**
**Check reported weather forecast perhaps (4)**

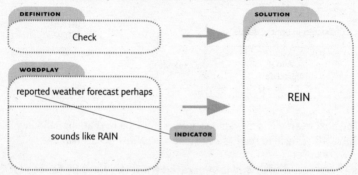

Some crosswords contain **self-referential** or **reverse homophones**; that is to say, the **homophone** is in the clue, rather than the solution. Here's an example of one:

**HOMOPHONE CLUE: Egg on a steak, say (4)**

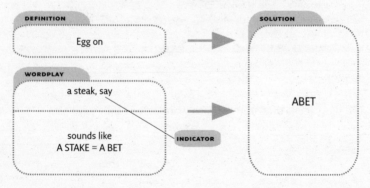

This is another **reverse homophone** which has the attraction of using alphabet letters in a novel way:

**HOMOPHONE CLUE: Characters in front of queue, say highly placed (4)**

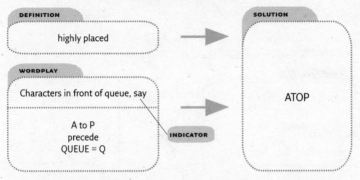

| DEFINITION | SOLUTION |
|---|---|
| highly placed | |
| **WORDPLAY** | ATOP |
| Characters in front of queue, say | |
| A to P precede QUEUE = Q | |
| INDICATOR | |

---

**TOP TIP – THE WORD *YOU***

A long-established extension of **reverse homophones** is that *you* may be used as a proxy for *you say* to give the letter *u* in part of the wordplay. A further more recent extension is provided by textspeak in which you = U, avoiding the need for a homophone indicator.

---

You may be stuck on a **homophone** clue because its sound to you is not the same as your pronunciation. The test for setters is whether the pronunciation is supported by one of the reference dictionaries (see Chapter 12) and I well know that setters receive complaints on this subject. Correspondents (especially from Scotland!) clearly dislike a homophone they do not relate to if the inference is that the setter's pronunciation is 'correct'. Ideally the indicator will reflect the fact that the pronunciation is not universal, as in, for example, *some may say*. However, the teaching point here is that solvers may occasionally need to be a little imaginative in their approach to homophone clues.

Finally, beware of clues which look as if they are **homophones** – you could easily be misled here by *said* in what is actually a **sandwich** clue:

**SANDWICH CLUE: It's said to include part of circuit (7)**

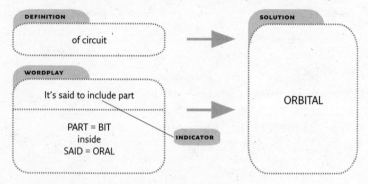

DEFINITION

of circuit

WORDPLAY

It's said to include part

PART = BIT
inside
SAID = ORAL

INDICATOR

SOLUTION

ORBITAL

## 4. The takeaway clue: finer points

It's not unusual for this clue type to be used alongside another, often anagrams. For example, the two types combine cleverly in this clue:

**TAKEAWAY CLUE: Skin and cook frozen duck (4)**

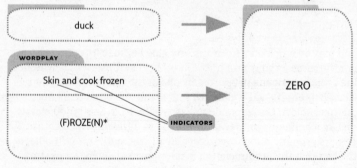

duck

WORDPLAY

Skin and cook frozen

(F)ROZE(N)*

INDICATORS

ZERO

The letters dropped, though often given by abbreviations, can be whole words:

**TAKEAWAY CLUE: Slight suspicion fish ejected black liquid (3)**

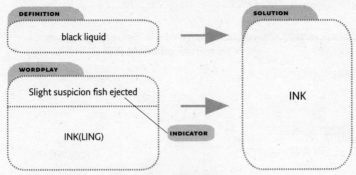

## 5. The hidden clue: finer points

The indicator may be at the end of the clue sentence as in the example below, in which the interpretation should be that a synonym of *zip* is being *employed* by the letters that follow it:

**HIDDEN CLUE: Zip fastener gymnast employs (6)**

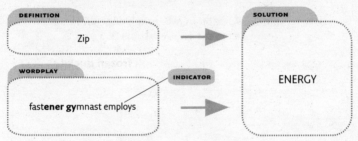

Also in a more difficult category, the solution can be spread over more than two words:

**HIDDEN CLUE: Wine to some extent features in a taverna (8)**

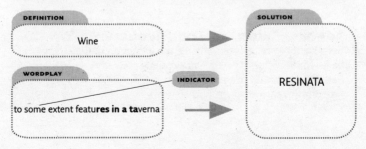

The letters concealed may have to be reversed before the solution is discovered, as here:

**HIDDEN AND REVERSAL CLUE: Swimmer turning in special pool (6)**

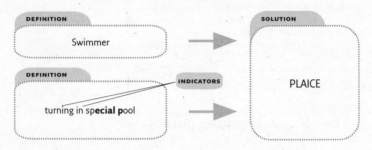

You should be on the lookout for very long and well-concealed solutions. This next wonderful effort must be just about the longest **hidden** clue that has appeared in a crossword:

**HIDDEN CLUE: As seen in jab, reach of pro miserably failing to meet expectations (6,2,7)**

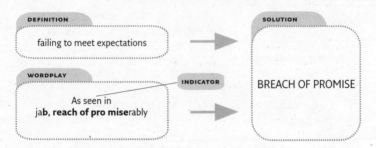

## TOP TIP – HIDDEN CLUE FREQUENCY

Because they are considered to be the easiest type, there may be no **hidden** clue in any one daily puzzle and rarely more than two or three. I refer to 15 by 15 square puzzles; there may well be proportionately more in jumbo-style puzzles.

Finally, for clues requiring the selection of alternate letters, it may be that not all the hidden letters form the whole solution. This is a combination of a **hidden** with an **additive** clue to demonstrate that point:

**HIDDEN AND ADDITIVE CLUE: From which spectators watch odd parts of their contest (7)**

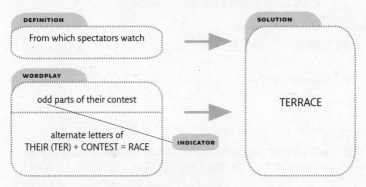

| DEFINITION | | SOLUTION |
| --- | --- | --- |
| From which spectators watch | → | |
| WORDPLAY | | TERRACE |
| odd parts of their contest | | |
| alternate letters of THEIR (TER) + CONTEST = RACE — INDICATOR | → | |

## 6. The reversal clue: finer points
Clues can be made up of reversals of more than one word. This one, with its nicely misleading definition, has two reversals:

**REVERSAL CLUE (DOWN CLUE): Exotic drama we're mounting – Butler did it (7)**

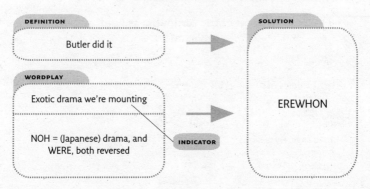

| DEFINITION | | SOLUTION |
| --- | --- | --- |
| Butler did it | → | |
| WORDPLAY | | EREWHON |
| Exotic drama we're mounting | | |
| NOH = (Japanese) drama, and WERE, both reversed — INDICATOR | → | |

Also in this category of clue, we include **palindromes**. Here's an elegant example:

**REVERSAL CLUE: Not an irreversible mistake (4)**

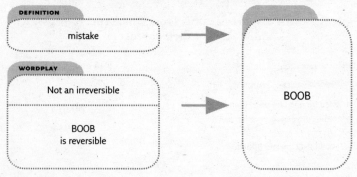

Other palindrome indicators could be: *looking both ways*, *whichever way you look at it*, *back and forth* (across clue), *up and down* (down clue).

## 7. The letter switch clue: finer points

The first example is similar to that in Chapter 3 where the letter to be switched is within the clue itself, whereas the second example is harder as the word to be manipulated must be found before the switch can be made:

**LETTER SWITCH CLUE: Antipathy as head of gallery replaced (7)**

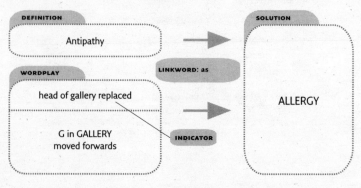

This second clue demonstrates the use of abbreviations, common for this clue type:

**LETTER SWITCH CLUE: Activity good for one on Pacific island (6)**

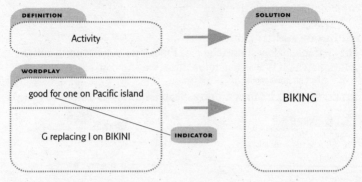

A change of direction may be required as in this nice clue:

**LETTER SWITCH CLUE: Soldiers go in here when grand old duke changes direction (4)**

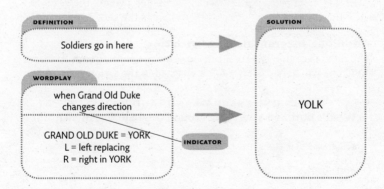

## 8. The all-in-one clue: finer points

This clue type has as many subsets as there are types of clue. In other words, the wordplay (remember: always the same as the definition, hence the term **all-in-one**) can take the form of an **anagram**, **additive** or any other sort. Indeed it can even be a combination of these. Here are some examples:

### All-in-one additive clue:

The example below shows the clue type at its most concise and the solution (which is a verb here) requires careful consideration:

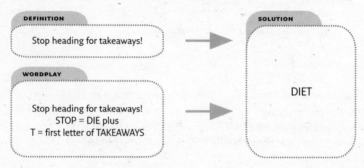

**ALL-IN-ONE ADDITIVE CLUE: Stop heading for takeaways! (4)**

DEFINITION

Stop heading for takeaways!

WORDPLAY

Stop heading for takeaways!
STOP = DIE plus
T = first letter of TAKEAWAYS

SOLUTION

DIET

### All-in-one anagram and sandwich clue:

The most common type of all-in-one clue is the **anagram**. Here's a good one which has a letter to be inserted in the **anagram fodder**:

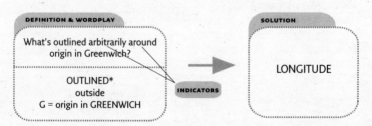

**ALL-IN-ONE ANAGRAM AND SANDWICH CLUE:
What's outlined arbitrarily around origin in Greenwich? (9)**

DEFINITION & WORDPLAY

What's outlined arbitrarily around origin in Greenwich?

OUTLINED*
outside
G = origin in GREENWICH

INDICATORS

SOLUTION

LONGITUDE

## All-in-one anagram and takeaway:

This involves an **anagram** and **takeaway** but is still eminently solvable – if you think comma after *actors*:

**ALL-IN-ONE ANAGRAM AND TAKEAWAY CLUE:**
**What could give actors no end of cachet? (5)**

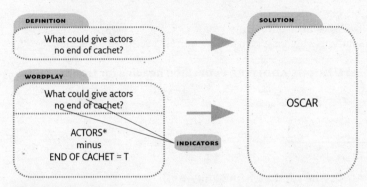

## All-in-one hidden:

The wordplay can be concealed neatly, as here, albeit that the answer word may have been replaced these days by a rucksack:

**ALL-IN-ONE HIDDEN CLUE: What's carried by pupils at Cheltenham? (7)**

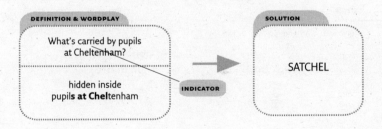

## All-in-one hidden and reversal:

The wordplay can also be hidden and reversed with a plural definition:

**ALL-IN-ONE HIDDEN AND REVERSAL CLUE:**
**They're found in returning perhaps to origins (5)**

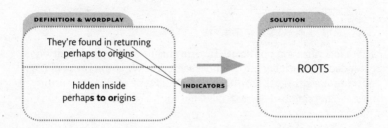

## All-in-one sandwich and anagram:

Finally, one of the most satisfying all-in-ones crafted by champion clue-writer Colin Dexter:

**ALL-IN-ONE SANDWICH AND ANAGRAM CLUE:**
**Item Gran arranged family slides in (5,7)**

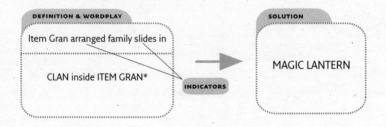

**IS THE ALL-IN-ONE CLUE THE MOST SATISFYING?**
Setters and judges of clue-writing contests tend to regard this sort
of clue as the pinnacle of clue-writing and it's true that all these
examples boast something special with their coincidence of definition
and wordplay. However, the **all-in-one** is not necessarily considered
so highly by the solvers I ask; their preference is a clue with a highly
misleading image and a pleasingly delayed penny-dropping. In addition,
the **all-in-one** may reveal its charms too quickly, especially in the case
of the subset discussed next.

There is a variation on the **all-in-one** clue in which the definition is
extended by wordplay into a whole sentence. We could think of it as
**partial** or a **semi all-in-one**. Solving this type of clue is in principle easier because of the extended definition. Here's one example:

**PARTIAL ALL-IN-ONE CLUE: Woman with veg cooking? (6)**

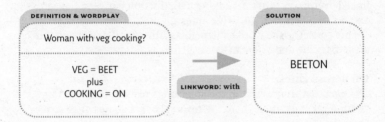

**LETTER FROM A SCHOOLBOY TO THE AUTHOR**
I have read your book *How to Crack Cryptic Crosswords*, which I found
really informative and have learnt a lot from. It has definitely improved
my skills and I will incorporate its information in my project.
Jonathan Levene, aged 13

Here's another example:

**PARTIAL ALL-IN-ONE CLUE: Show with nude in naughty act? (7)**

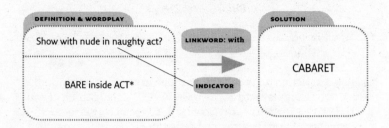

## 9. The additive clue: finer points

Some crosswords, notably *The Times*, follow a convention established over many years in making a distinction between the across and down position in **additive** clues.

This concerns the word *on* which, as a linkword, means *after* in an across clue and *before* in a down clue, as set out next.

**For across clues:**

The part that comes first in the solution is placed second in the wordplay. For example, here the reversal of *kin* comes after *strike = beat*:

**ADDITIVE CLUE INCL. REVERSAL (ACROSS): Bohemian family goes back on strike (7)**

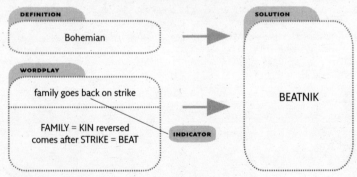

**For down clues:**

In down clues the parts keep the order of the clue sentence, as with the *was* preceding the *sail = canvas* in this:

**ADDITIVE CLUE (DOWN): Festive occasion was put on canvas (7)**

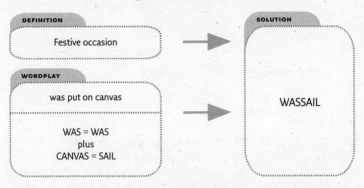

Sometimes the solution word can be broken down into separate parts to form the wordplay. Solving these clues is often a question of working from the definition back to the wordplay:

**ADDITIVE CLUE: Cold display unit for seafood (11)**

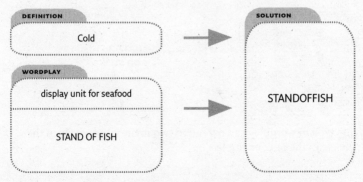

Finally, it will bear repetition from Chapter 3 that the order of the letters or words to be combined may have to be switched, as in the next clue:

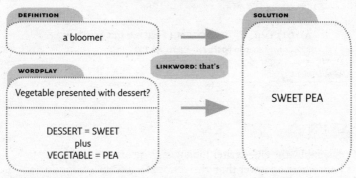

## 10. The cryptic definition clue: finer points

The more instinctive solver finds this clue one of the easiest; others like me find it the hardest and my practice, once I have recognized the type, is to leave it till later when some solution letters are available. This is especially so when the information given is minimal, as here in a humorous clue:

**CRYPTIC DEFINITION CLUE: In which three couples get together for sex (5)**

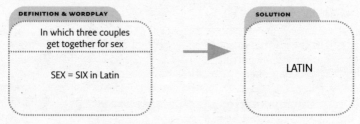

This type of wordplay can extend to two misleading words in the clue, as in the next example:

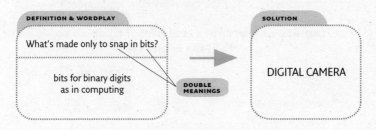

**CRYPTIC DEFINITION CLUE: What's made only to snap in bits? (7,6)**

DEFINITION & WORDPLAY

What's made only to snap in bits?

bits for binary digits as in computing

DOUBLE MEANINGS

SOLUTION

DIGITAL CAMERA

Occasionally the clue-writer manages to be exceptionally cryptic as here where no fewer than three words have misleading surface meanings:

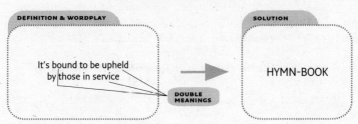

**CRYPTIC DEFINITION CLUE: It's bound to be upheld by those in service (4-4)**

DEFINITION & WORDPLAY

It's bound to be upheld by those in service

DOUBLE MEANINGS

SOLUTION

HYMN-BOOK

Finally, it is essential to consider each word closely as the solution may be unlocked by putting emphasis on a seemingly unimportant part of the clue, as here:

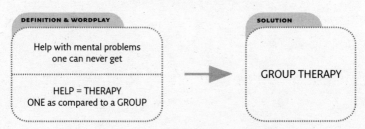

**CRYPTIC DEFINITION CLUE: Help with mental problems one can never get (5,7)**

DEFINITION & WORDPLAY

Help with mental problems one can never get

HELP = THERAPY
ONE as compared to a GROUP

SOLUTION

GROUP THERAPY

## 11. The double definition clue: finer points

While these can be recognized from their brevity when there are only two words side by side, they can be longer and harder to spot:

**DOUBLE DEFINITION CLUE: A lot of criminals go north of the border (4)**

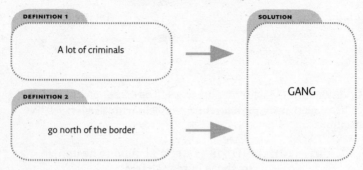

**DEFINITION 1**

A lot of criminals

**DEFINITION 2**

go north of the border

**SOLUTION**

GANG

Also note that there may be one of several possible linkwords eg *for*, *in* or *is* between the two or more definitions as below:

**DOUBLE DEFINITION CLUE: Responsibility for tax (4)**

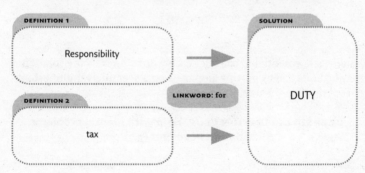

**DEFINITION 1**

Responsibility

**DEFINITION 2**

tax

**LINKWORD: for**

**SOLUTION**

DUTY

## DOUBLE DEFINITION CLUE: **Back in a moment (6)**

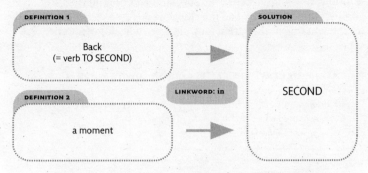

| DEFINITION 1 | | SOLUTION |
|---|---|---|
| Back (= verb TO SECOND) | → | |
| | LINKWORD: in | SECOND |
| DEFINITION 2 | | |
| a moment | → | |

## DOUBLE DEFINITION CLUE: **Expert is over (12)**

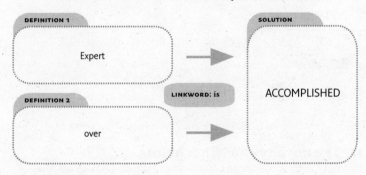

| DEFINITION 1 | | SOLUTION |
|---|---|---|
| Expert | → | |
| | LINKWORD: is | ACCOMPLISHED |
| DEFINITION 2 | | |
| over | → | |

Double definition clues may have a cryptic element in one or other of their parts. Witness this clue:

## DOUBLE DEFINITION CLUE: **Where to see Tommy eating pickle (4)**

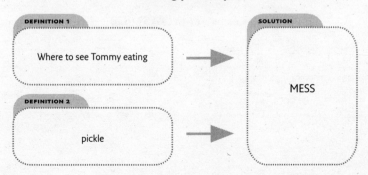

| DEFINITION 1 | | SOLUTION |
|---|---|---|
| Where to see Tommy eating | → | |
| | | MESS |
| DEFINITION 2 | | |
| pickle | → | |

Finally, an example of three definitions which exploit a word with multiple meanings. There is no special tip for finding your way through this ingenious and mischievous wording other than to note that it contains nothing that looks like an indicator of another clue type:

**TRIPLE DEFINITION CLUE: Kentish Town's wood trade (4)**

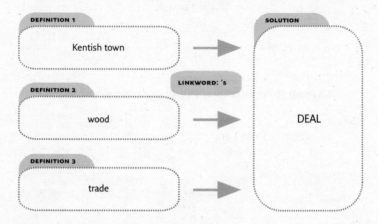

DEFINITION 1 — Kentish town → SOLUTION

LINKWORD: 's

DEFINITION 2 — wood → DEAL

DEFINITION 3 — trade →

## 12. The novelty clue: finer points

By their very nature, these clues defy generalized advice on solving them. There may or may not be an indicator, and there may be an exclamation mark to signal something extraordinary. Otherwise it's a question of thinking laterally. The first is the "clue" everyone seems to know. Lacking a definition and not having any surface meaning doesn't hold it back in people's affection:

**NOVELTY CLUE: GGES? (9,4)**

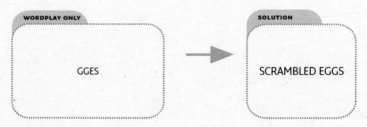

WORDPLAY ONLY — GGES → SOLUTION — SCRAMBLED EGGS

Much better because it has a definition is:

**NOVELTY CLUE: CIVIC figures (5,8)**

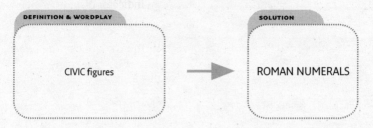

Now for a really innovative clue, as indicated by the exclamation mark:

**NOVELTY CLUE: Landmines when suitably spaced could do for these trees! (4)**

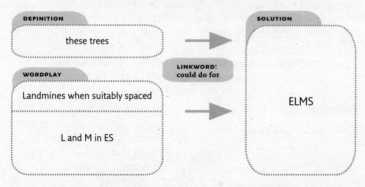

Next, you must split the solution into two parts and imagine it as a slogan supporting the Queen.

## NOVELTY CLUE: Servant's anti-republican slogan? (8)

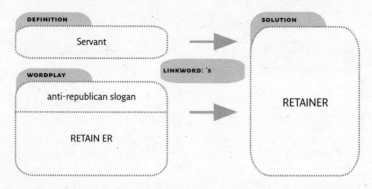

**DEFINITION**
Servant

**LINKWORD: 's**

**WORDPLAY**
anti-republican slogan

RETAIN ER

**SOLUTION**
RETAINER

Under this heading we can include clues which use the verbal twisting of William Archibald Spooner. He was an Anglican clergyman and Warden of New College, Oxford, whose nervous manner led him to utter many slips of the tongue, notably involving comic reversals such as Queer old Dean for Dear old Queen. This is an example of a clue in this style:

## NOVELTY CLUE: Lowest possible cost of jam and cereal for Spooner (7,5)

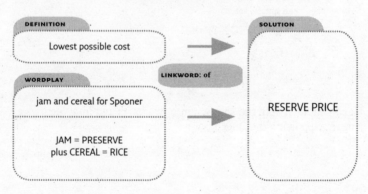

**DEFINITION**
Lowest possible cost

**LINKWORD: of**

**WORDPLAY**
jam and cereal for Spooner

JAM = PRESERVE
plus CEREAL = RICE

**SOLUTION**
RESERVE PRICE

Finally, the briefest possible clue of any kind that may appeal to romantic tennis fans:

## NOVELTY CLUE: O? (4,6)

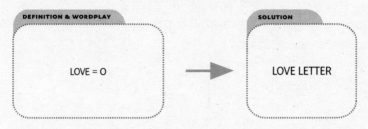

DEFINITION & WORDPLAY

LOVE = O

SOLUTION

LOVE LETTER

**TIMES LEADER**
The crossword reminds readers that, amid the strife and controversy of today's headlines, there really is, in one part of the newpaper, at least a definitive and elegant solution.

# 9. Finer Points of Clues: General

> *"I attempted yesterday's* Times *crossword and managed to complete three clues – quid, Turgenev and courtier. I can only improve."*
> Lord Archer, *A Prison Diary*

Now to some points that are unrelated to specific clue types.

## 1. Complex constructions
Until now we have been concerned with demonstrating how to solve clues that have one or two elements of trickery within them. Most clues do follow this pattern but should you be daunted by those which have even more? I'd say not at all: it's still a question of decoding the separate elements, each of which will be signalled in its own way. Even if the word defined is an unusual one and the wordplay complex, you follow the indicators eventually to arrive at the solution. The complex clue is reserved usually for intractable words (as in the following example), for which the setter can find no alternative. Don't worry if you find this too unreasonably difficult (I do, too!) as simplicity is the ideal of most setters – a clue like this is thankfully rare:

**COMPLEX CLUE – SANDWICH INCLUDING REVERSAL AND HOMOPHONE: Intense campaign's settled audience's worries reflected in petition (10)**

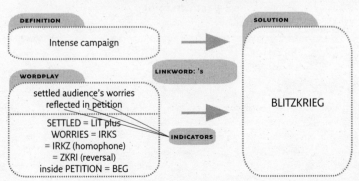

DEFINITION

Intense campaign

WORDPLAY

settled audience's worries reflected in petition

SETTLED = LIT plus
WORRIES = IRKS
= IRKZ (homophone)
= ZKRI (reversal)
inside PETITION = BEG

LINKWORD: 's

INDICATORS

SOLUTION

BLITZKRIEG

## 2. Linkwords

Fairly commonly, the linkword has to be taken as one form in the surface reading and a different form in the cryptic reading. In this example, the use of *'s* means possessive pronoun in the former and *is* in the latter.

**SANDWICH CLUE: Moll's 'leave it alone' as bottom's pinched (8)**

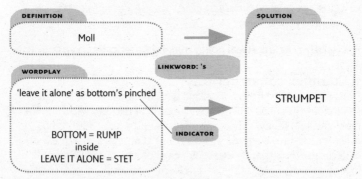

DEFINITION

Moll

WORDPLAY

'leave it alone' as bottom's pinched

BOTTOM = RUMP
inside
LEAVE IT ALONE = STET

LINKWORD: 's

INDICATOR

SOLUTION

STRUMPET

## 3. Punctuation: misleading

Apart from question marks and exclamation marks (see next paragraph), punctuation is by convention in all crosswords unreliable. This is especially confusing to beginners who have to be reminded that it may mislead and may have to be ignored. For example, as mentioned before, the components of an anagram can be split across a full stop or a comma.

**ANAGRAM CLUE: Composition of Lennon, voice of pacifism (3-8)**

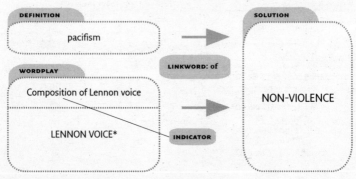

DEFINITION

pacifism

WORDPLAY

Composition of Lennon voice

LENNON VOICE*

LINKWORD: of

INDICATOR

SOLUTION

NON-VIOLENCE

## TOP TIP – DIRECTION OF LINKWORDS

Working out which way the linkword is pointing can be tricky. For example, while it is entirely normal (in normal English and crosswords) that *from* and *leading to* point to the answer from the preceding wordplay, the reverse may occasionally apply. The test is whether the wordplay stands for the definition: that is to say, it clearly and grammatically shows the process which gives the solution. By stretching the language, some linkwords such as *get*, *gets*, *getting*, *makes* or *making* can point either way. Here is an example:

**ANAGRAM CLUE: Fiscal policy making Americans go wrong? (11)**

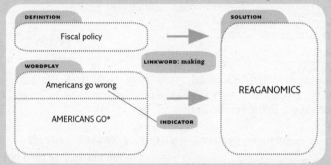

You are required to think of the solution giving rise to the **anagram fodder**. The reverse order, as in my reworked clue below, would be more natural and is more likely to be found in the best puzzles.

**ANAGRAM CLUE: Americans go wrong making fiscal policy (11)**

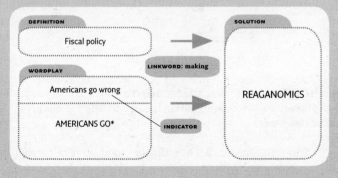

Or punctuation can mislead by separating the parts to be manipulated, as seen here:

**ADDITIVE CLUE: Cold potato? Fine (5)**

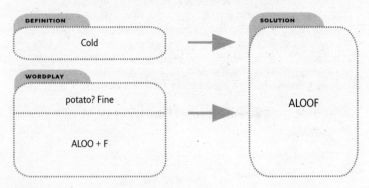

Punctuation can be omitted, too, as here where the comma required by the cryptic reading between the last two words (as in 'I, say') is not shown in the second definition:

**DOUBLE DEFINITION CLUE: 'Excellent', I say (7)**

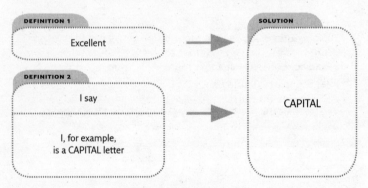

## 4. Punctuation: not misleading
The exceptions when punctuation is there to help are mainly in these two cases:

- **Question mark**: as a hint that the solution either is slightly tenuous, or it's an example of a group rather than a synonym.

**TOP TIP – WHAT DO ELLIPSES IN CLUES MEAN?**
The answer is simple: it's merely a way of connecting two clues (sometimes more) to present a longer than normal clue sentence, i.e. across the two clues. Each clue stands on its own with regard to definition and wordplay (even if one part references another). Here is an example in which the first is an **anagram** and the second an **additive**:

**TWO CLUES LINKED BY ELLIPSES:**
**5 down: Indian pipe made from a cut elm… (7)**

**6 down: …a small hard tree (3)**

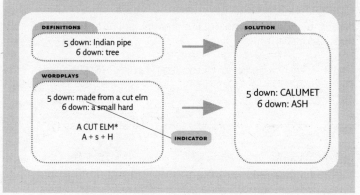

Thus *apple* to define *fruit* may well have a question mark.
- **Exclamation mark**: as an indication either that something most unusual is going on within the clue, or that the clue has a remarkable or humorous feature that the setter wants you especially to notice, albeit not in a self-congratulatory manner.

Occasionally, punctuation is included to make the deciphering of the wordplay clearer, as in the next clue in which the exclamation mark helps to identify or confirm the answer.

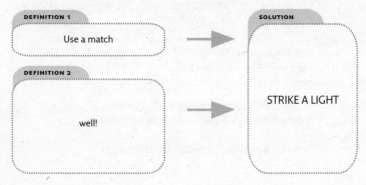

Finally, here is an example of punctuation not only being helpful but forming the definition:

**ADDITIVE CLUE: Argue score? (8,4)**

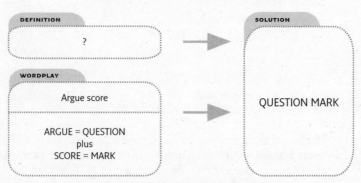

I would not be surprised if you are somewhat discombobulated by the points in the above section. They are undoubtedly tricky but I'm sure you will eventually find punctuation no major problem.

## 5. More deceptive linkwords

In section 2 of this chapter we saw one deceptive use of the 's. The clue below shows another. The apostrophe looks at first glance as though it may be a **linkword** (for *is*) but in fact it's an adjectival synonym for the solution.

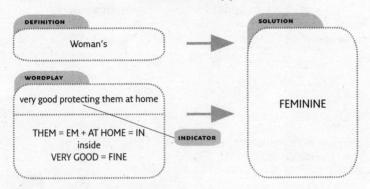

**SANDWICH CLUE: Woman's very good protecting them at home (8)**

DEFINITION

Woman's

SOLUTION

FEMININE

WORDPLAY

very good protecting them at home

THEM = EM + AT HOME = IN
inside
VERY GOOD = FINE

INDICATOR

# 6. Crossword war horses

There are inevitably some crossword terms that occur time and again, often words of two, three or four letters. It is impossible to list all of them here but those in this P. G. Wodehouse quotation (from *Meet Mr Mulliner*) may still be seen today:

> 'George spent his evenings doing the crossword puzzle. By the time he was thirty he knew more about Eli, the prophet, Ra the Sun God and the bird Emu than anybody else in the country except the vicar's daughter who had also taken up the solving of crossword puzzles and was the first girl in Worcestershire to find out the meaning of stearine and crepuscular.'

A military war horse is an American Civil War General still honoured in crosswords, as in this next clue:

**SANDWICH CLUE: General secures unit some drink (8)**

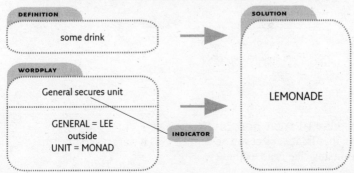

DEFINITION

some drink

SOLUTION

LEMONADE

WORDPLAY

General secures unit

GENERAL = LEE
outside
UNIT = MONAD

INDICATOR

A car last produced in 1927 remains a favourite reference:

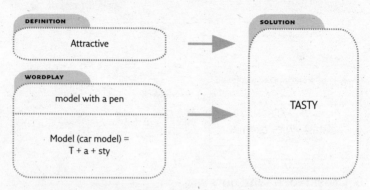

**ADDITIVE CLUE: Attractive model with a pen (5)**

DEFINITION: Attractive

WORDPLAY: model with a pen

Model (car model) = T + a + sty

SOLUTION: TASTY

I also note that all journalists can be ranked as Ed; that the only races known to some setters are motorcycle races TT and that the old-fashioned STEAMSHIP still sails as SS, notably in popular sandwich clues as "on board" ie with S first and last.

## 7. Stuttering clues
A sentence uttered stutteringly is indicated by repetition, as follows:

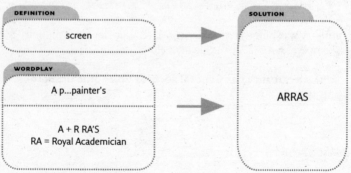

**ADDITIVE CLUE: A p...painter's screen (5)**

DEFINITION: screen

WORDPLAY: A p...painter's

A + R RA'S
RA = Royal Academician

SOLUTION: ARRAS

## 8. Use of first person singular
An inanimate object can be defined as if it were a person. This amusing clue is an example:

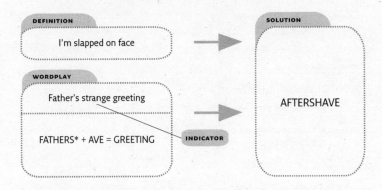

**ANAGRAM AND ADDITIVE CLUE:**
**Father's strange greeting – I'm slapped on face (10)**

DEFINITION

I'm slapped on face

WORDPLAY

Father's strange greeting

FATHERS* + AVE = GREETING

INDICATOR

SOLUTION

AFTERSHAVE

## 9. Living people

Some newspapers are cautious with regard to clues referring to or defining people still alive. They are happy with this beauty about former VIPs:

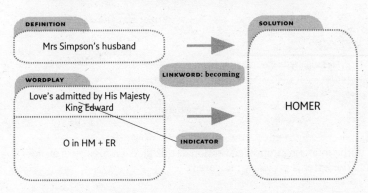

**SANDWICH CLUE: Love's admitted by His Majesty**
**King Edward, becoming Mrs Simpson's husband (5)**

DEFINITION

Mrs Simpson's husband

LINKWORD: becoming

WORDPLAY

Love's admitted by His Majesty King Edward

O in HM + ER

INDICATOR

SOLUTION

HOMER

The practice though, notably in the *Guardian*, the *Independent* and *Private Eye*, is to revel in clues such as this one about a living person:

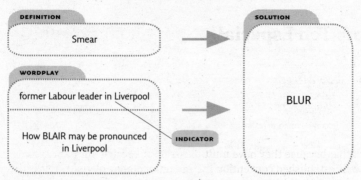

## 10. Misleading positioning of indicators

The letter selection indicator is sometimes not ideally positioned, as with *initially* below. Solvers have to try both M and N as letters in anagram fodder.

**ANAGRAM CLUE: Virgin Media initially not working (6)**

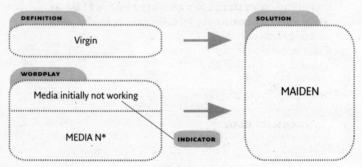

In the following improved version of this clue, ambiguity is avoided as the letter N is clearly indicated:

**ANAGRAM CLUE: Virgin Media not initially working (6)**

# 10. Ten Especially Troublesome Words

*"My agent rings, she says: 'I'm stuck on the crossword. The clue's "Overloaded postman".' I pause a moment: 'How many letters?' 'Hundreds.'"*

Jeremy Paxman, *Spectator* diary

Either because they have multiple uses, or because they are a well-established convention but not immediately obvious, there are a few particularly awkward words which it's good to know about. The first two, *about* and *in*, are especially difficult for newcomers.

## 1. About

One of the most misleading words in crosswords is *about* because it has so many uses:

- a **reversal** indicator of whole words, or parts of them, in across and down clues
- a **sandwich** indicator
- an **anagram** indicator
- *C*, *CA* as abbreviations
- a synonym for *re* and *on*

You'd be forgiven for thinking this is a sandwich clue, but it isn't:

**ANAGRAM CLUE: Wrote about tall building (5)**

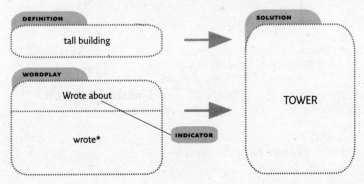

DEFINITION

tall building

WORDPLAY

Wrote about

wrote*

INDICATOR

SOLUTION

TOWER

## 2. In

Likewise the innocent little multi-purpose word *in* causes trouble. Each of these next clues uses *in* differently. First, as a **hidden** indicator:

### HIDDEN CLUE: **Happy perhaps, in battlefield warfare (5)**

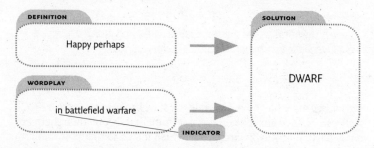

DEFINITION
Happy perhaps

WORDPLAY
in battlefield warfare

INDICATOR

SOLUTION
DWARF

Second, as a **linkword** between definition and wordplay:

### ADDITIVE CLUE: **Be prolific in area before spring (6)**

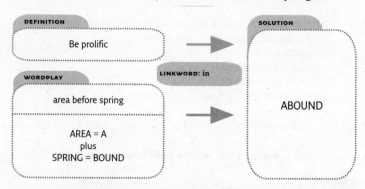

DEFINITION
Be prolific

LINKWORD: in

WORDPLAY
area before spring

AREA = A
plus
SPRING = BOUND

SOLUTION
ABOUND

**LETTERS TO THE TIMES**
Sir, Your reporting staff deserve a medal for enduring the rabble that took place in the House of Commons yesterday... I turned the TV off and got on with the crosswords.

Third, as a **sandwich** indicator:

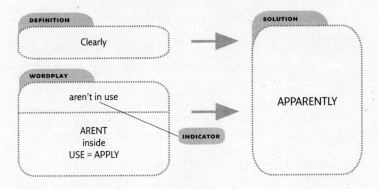

**SANDWICH CLUE: Clearly aren't in use (10)**

DEFINITION

Clearly

WORDPLAY

aren't in use

ARENT
inside
USE = APPLY

INDICATOR

SOLUTION

APPARENTLY

Fourth (though rarely), as a **definition**:

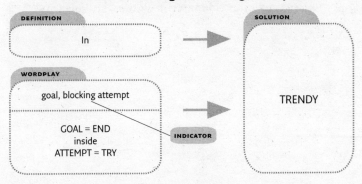

**SANDWICH CLUE: In goal, blocking attempt (6)**

DEFINITION

In

WORDPLAY

goal, blocking attempt

GOAL = END
inside
ATTEMPT = TRY

INDICATOR

SOLUTION

TRENDY

Fifth (equally rarely), as a **definition** in another language:

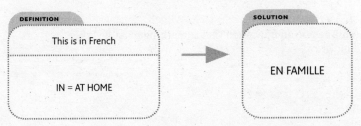

**CRYPTIC DEFINITION: This is in French (2,7)**

DEFINITION

This is in French

IN = AT HOME

SOLUTION

EN FAMILLE

Sixth, as part of the **definition**:

**HOMOPHONE CLUE: One in bed reciting numbers of sheep (5)**

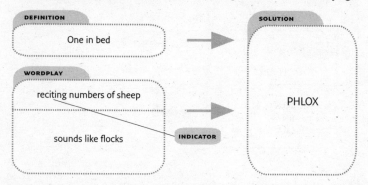

Seventh, as part of the **wordplay**:

**ADDITIVE CLUE: Monarch in clothes, striking (9)**

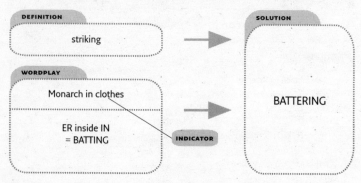

The first, second and third of these usages are by far the most common.

## 3. Without

This can be an indication that something must be taken away, as below:

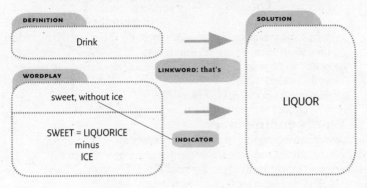

**TAKEAWAY CLUE: Drink that's sweet, without ice (6)**

DEFINITION

Drink

LINKWORD: that's

WORDPLAY

sweet, without ice

SWEET = LIQUORICE
minus
ICE

INDICATOR

SOLUTION

LIQUOR

In some puzzles, *without* is also still used in the sense of *outside* (marked as archaic in most dictionaries). It is therefore a **sandwich** indicator, as follows:

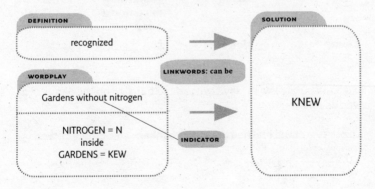

**SANDWICH CLUE: Gardens without nitrogen can be recognized (4)**

DEFINITION

recognized

LINKWORDS: can be

WORDPLAY

Gardens without nitrogen

NITROGEN = N
inside
GARDENS = KEW

INDICATOR

SOLUTION

KNEW

## 4. One
The word *one* can be a **wordplay** substitute for *I*, *ace*, *a*, *an* and *un* (from the dialect usage *'un*).

## 5. Men

In cryptics, men do demonstrate an ability to multi-task:

- *man* can be *he*, a chess piece or pawn, a soldier, an island as in the Isle of Man, or just a plain fellow
- *male* can be *m* or *he* (which as HE – His Excellency – is also an ambassador)
- *men* can be *or* (for *other ranks*)

## 6. Words ending in -er

In the sometimes artificial world of crosswords, we can encounter nouns with unexpected, sometimes unnatural, not to say groan-worthy, meanings that are implied rather than actually specified in dictionaries.

Here are some examples:

| | | | |
|---|---|---|---|
| river or stream | *flower* | bird | *winger* |
| anaesthetist | *number* | ram | *butter* |
| cow | *lower* | competitor | *strainer* |
| fish | *swimmer* | something in compost heap | *rotter* |
| lamp | *glower* | sun | *setter* |

So a banker may live in, say, Switzerland but also on the banks of a river, as follows:

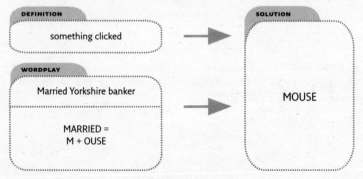

**ADDITIVE CLUE: Married Yorkshire banker – something clicked (5)**

| DEFINITION | SOLUTION |
|---|---|
| something clicked | |
| **WORDPLAY** | MOUSE |
| Married Yorkshire banker | |
| MARRIED = M + OUSE | |

## 7. Of

*Of* can very occasionally be a linking word between the definition and wordplay. Its meaning in this case is stretched (arguably too far) to *from* or *constituted by* as here in this example:

**ANAGRAM CLUE: Developed new part of Belgian city (7)**

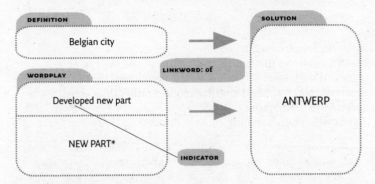

## 8 & 9. Right and left

*Right* and *left* appear in a number of guises. *Right* can be an **anagram** indicator (= verb, *to correct*); the letter *r* as an abbreviation; and synonyms such as *ok* and *lien*. *Left* can be a **takeaway** indicator; the abbreviation *l*; and synonyms such as *over* and *port*.

## 10. Say

As well as its most common usage as a synonym for *for example* or *e.g.*, the word *say* can indicate a **homophone**, as in the first clue below, or it can be a simple synonym, as in the second:

**HOMOPHONE CLUE: Shrub or trees, say (5)**

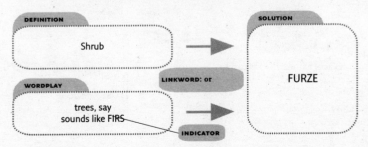

**ALL-IN-ONE ADDITIVE CLUE: One to produce key, say (6)**

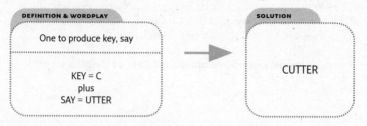

DEFINITION & WORDPLAY

One to produce key, say

KEY = C
plus
SAY = UTTER

SOLUTION

CUTTER

> **TOP TIP – KEY NOTES**
> The word *key* (as in the previous clue) and its sister, *note*, can have a lot of forms in their various musical guises. As regards phonetic notes, they are these: *do, doh, re, mi, me, fa, so, soh, la, lah, te, ti*; or they can be single letters: *a, b, c, d, e, f, g*. Despite this unwanted luxury of choice, you should normally find that clues with any of these references leave you in no doubt which note is required.

## 11. To

By now you know that clues do not contain words without any purpose. A common exception is inclusion of the word *to* before verbs. I'm unsure why so let's call it a long-standing convention. Here's an example in which the first *to* is superfluous but the second is fair since it forms part of the build-up:

**ADDITIVE CLUE: Official has to fix period to run in the cooler (12)**

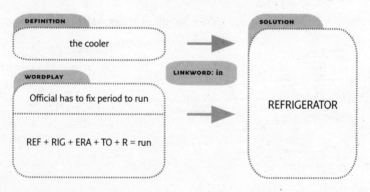

DEFINITION

the cooler

WORDPLAY

Official has to fix period to run

REF + RIG + ERA + TO + R = run

LINKWORD: in

SOLUTION

REFRIGERATOR

**LETTERS TO THE TIMES**

Sir, it is always a joy for me when England play Test cricket. Pictures on the back page allow me more uncluttered white areas to do my anagrams.
Henry Pottle

# 11: Ten Ways to Raise Your Game

> "Reporters observed Mrs Attlee's eccentric driving as the Prime
> Minister busied himself with crosswords in the back of his car."
> Kevin Jeffrey, *Finest and Darkest Hours*

We will now look at methods that you might consider for improving
your crossword-solving skills.

## 1. Practice, practice, practice!

This is the number one recommendation for improvement. There
are many verbal tricks and conventions that are more easily recognized after you have done lots of crosswords. That still leaves
room for setters to provide new ones, so have no fear that boredom
will set in! You may like to practise by trying some of the clues and
puzzles later in the book.

## 2. Solve with a friend

People often tell me that they enjoy doing all or part of the puzzle
with a family member or work colleague. This can be face-to-face or
by the many electronic ways available but whichever is used, there
seems to be a significant solving improvement. Incidentally, after one
of my workshops, the participants formed an internet-based group
to help each other solve their daily crossword and this has spread
to University of the Third Age (aka U3A, a thriving organisation for
retired folk), some of which have more than one crossword group.

## 3. Join an online crossword club

The best of these are run by *The Times*, *Daily Telegraph* and *Guardian*
(includes the *Observer*), the *Irish Times* and there is a flourishing
Australian Crossword Club.

Most of these understandably require a small annual payment in
return for which archived puzzles as well as current crosswords are
available for practice.

In addition there is the very first crossword club run since inception by
Brian Head based in Awbridge, Hampshire providing a monthly mainly
online magazine of puzzles, clue writing contests and other goodies.

## 4. Buy a book of crosswords

If good old-fashioned books are what you prefer, then one of the large number available may appeal. There are books for many of the puzzles mentioned in this book.

## 5. Enjoy a fun workshop

Strictly non-competitive, open to all of any age and whatever existing skills, a crossword workshop is a proven way to improve skills and experience. Details of those coming up in your area are available on various websites, including the author's at *www.timmoorey.info*. The first of these has run at the very successful and friendly Marlborough College Summer School in Wiltshire since 2006 and takes place on weekday mornings in July.

### Residential
Marlborough: www.mcsummerschool.org.uk
Somerset: www.dillington.com

### Non-residential
London: www.howtoacademy.com

## 6. Try the Monday crossword

True or not, many solvers tell me that Monday crosswords are the easiest of the week. If so, it's not by design, I suspect but the belief could give newcomers a confidence boost!

## 7. Study the published solutions

Though explanations are not published, it can be highly productive to study the solutions published and to work backwards for any clues you have not managed to crack. I believe many would like to see annotated solutions but space limitations prevail.

## 8. Study the blogs

These are covered in Chapter 12.

## 9. Study the website www.andlit.org.uk

Maintained by John Tozer, this site is a treasure trove of prize-winning clues from the *Observer*'s Azed competition which began in 1972. Whilst the Azed crossword is of the barred type not covered here, hundreds of clues should make for a stimulating read and the commentary by Azed and indeed Ximenes himself in their "slips" will give many further insights into best practice principles.

# WHAT DISTINGUISHES THE LIBERTARIAN SCHOOL FROM THE XIMENEAN ONE?

It would take a lot of space to comment on this and I suspect many readers would not want to stay with me. A few examples will suffice. Libertarian clues may require the solver to split words like *indeed* into *in* and *deed* where, say, *part* is to be inserted to make the answer *departed*. You may also be required to stretch normal word meanings, as in an imaginative definition of composer Vivaldi. He has been clued as a 'seasonal barman'. This seems slightly degrading for the Red Priest but amusing nonetheless. Wagner has been similarly clued in a single word without further wordplay as 'Ringmaster (6)'.

Slight stretching of homophones for comic effect will be found.
For example:
*To make cheese, how do you milk a Welsh hedgehog? (10)*
*Answer: Caerphilly*

Hidden clues may have superfluous words and disregard reality:
*Most Richard Tauber records contain this bird (7)*
*Answer: ostrich*

Single word clues may need splitting as here:
*Ascribe? (8,5)*
*Answer: articled clerk*

Indicators may be missing as in the reversal needed here:
*Announcement to put into a French resort (6)*
*Answer: notice*

Rules of grammar are usually obeyed but not always:
*A nut go into this (6)*
*Answer: nougat*
To make it worse for Ximeneans, this clue also lacks a proper anagram indicator according to the precepts explained earlier.

Where would you find this type of clueing? Principally from some but by no means all setters in the *Guardian* where all the above clues appeared. However *Guardian* readers know what to expect and clearly greatly enjoy this *Anything Goes* school of clue-writing. They may well agree with the sentiment expressed by one solver to me that crosswords need to develop and should not be bound by a stickler classics master of over 50 years ago.

## 10. Enjoy *Cracking the Cryptic* on YouTube

Mark Goodliffe (also see page 123) and Simon Anthony demonstrate their real time solving of a cryptic. Well worth watching!

**SPEED SOLVING CHAMPION'S TIPS**

Mark Goodliffe, who typically solves three Times puzzles in 20 minutes, has won the Times championship 11 times. Here are his tips (as provided for a BBC Radio 4 programme):

1 Some of the words in the clue may only be there to provide their letters, not their meaning.
2 Each puzzle will contain a variety of wordplay: a few anagrams, and then a mix of definitions, reversals, hidden words or homophones. Try and find the ones you prefer.
3 There are THREE ways to get a solution: definition, wordplay and letters already in the grid.
4 Learn the valid single letter abbreviations.
5 Anything in the clue might mislead: the apparent surface meaning, punctuation, even how a word appears to sound eg flower meaning something that flows.
6 Get used to some of the very standard crossword usages eg initially (first letter), regularly (every other letter of), and anagram indicators.
7 There are one or two exceptions to the clue types: cryptic definition (misleading definitions) and & lit clues where the whole clue acts as both wordplay and definition.

NB. "& lit" known as "all-in-one" in this book.

**PART 3**

# PRACTICE TIME

## 12: Recommended Books, Websites & Media

> *"Unlike crossword fanatics I do actually read the paper."*
> Bernice Rubens

There's much more help available than just a dictionary these days as an increasing number of books, websites and electronic gadgets offer assistance. Here are some recommendations:

### 1. Dictionaries
The principal dictionaries used by setters today for blocked crosswords are *Collins English Dictionary*, the *Concise Oxford Dictionary* and *Chambers*, the latter being the source par excellence for barred crosswords. Occasionally bigger dictionaries in the Oxford family may need to be consulted for top-end cryptics. Note that Collins has names of people (which it once didn't).

### 2. Thesauruses
Collins, Oxford and Chambers all publish useful dictionaries of synonyms and all three are more efficient for crossword solvers than the longer established *Roget's Thesaurus*, the use of which can involve lots of page-turning for any one reference.

### 3. Word list books
**Collins Bradford's Crossword Solver's Dictionary (2018)**
This has been the book of choice among the crossword public for over forty years, principally because of its method of production. Not having been compiled from computerized lists, it was, and continues to be, built up by its author, Anne Bradford, from solutions actually appearing in a variety of crosswords. That means you have a good chance of finding the name of, say, that elusive horse (well over 200 entries) to complete the puzzle.

**Chambers Crossword Dictionary, 4th edition, 2016**
This nicely complements *Bradford's*, as well as containing extra
features, e.g. articles on crossword English, indicators and what
constitutes a good clue. It is rare for an answer word in a daily not
to be found in either of these two books, both of which are published in cheaper, pocket-sized editions.

## 4. Electronic aids – pocket machines
### Sharp PWE300 or 500A
This includes the *Oxford Dictionary*, the *Oxford Thesaurus* and, in
the case of the PWE500A, the *Oxford Dictionary of Quotations*, all
searchable by individual words and phrases.Like the pocket
machine recommended next, it has anagram and word search facilities. Thus, if you need to find a four-letter word ending in *j* you will
do so easily and quickly. I have used the PWE500 (now PWE500A)
for several years instead of carrying dictionaries and wordlist books
around. However, smartphone users can now access most of this
and similar material easily and cheaply (see next section), perhaps
accounting for the recent poor availability of this machine. If you
find it unavailable, I'd suggest you try eBay or one of the Seiko
equivalents that contain the *Concise Oxford Dictionary*.

### Franklin
There are many good electronic machines available in this range.

## 5. Electronic aids – apps for tablets and smartphones
As well as many downloadable dictionaries and thesauruses from,
say, Oxford and Merriam-Webster, there are many effective and
inexpensive smartphone and tablet apps on all platforms. Typing
*crossword* into Google's Play store and the iPhone's equivalent will
produce a good choice. As an Android user, the one I recommend
is *crossword solver* by Havos Limited but there are others, normally
free. The iPhone equivalents are *the crossword solver* and *crossword*,
both also free.

The *Chambers Dictionary* and *Thesaurus* apps are inexpensive,
comprehensive and have excellent search facilities, including
wildcard searches. I have used both for years and find they are now
usually my first choice as solving aids.

If you are looking for a free app including dictionary, thesaurus
and word search, WordWeb, available in many formats, is the one
to go for.

**DID YOU KNOW?**
One crossword setter in the 1960s, wishing to include the word *miniskirt* in a puzzle, found that the word had not yet been added to the *Chambers Dictionary*, and came up with this delightful clue:

*"Female attire not to be found in* Chambers, *but should not be looked up anyway."*

## 6. Online dictionaries, word search and reference

If you don't have one of the electronic aids listed above, and fancy a spot of "cheating", Collins, Oxford and Chambers all have word search facilities online. Also you may be unaware that the biggest of them all, the *Oxford English Dictionary* (the *OED*) may be available without charge online by using your local library card.

The biggest online but not necessarily the best (as it does not include some well-known dictionaries such as *Chambers*) may be at *www.onelook.com* which combines the content of over 1000 dictionaries. This passed my test using the words *keraunograph* and *taghairm* with flying colours.

For all its well-reported weaknesses in terms of reliability, Wikipedia's comprehensiveness makes it excellent if you want a quick check on a factual solution. I use it regularly as my reference of online choice and can't remember it letting me down. Rather, mistakes that have occurred in my own crosswords are likely to have arisen because I have not consulted Wikipedia.

You might also try *www.bestforpuzzles.com*, a site which has a huge variety of help tools, one of which is the daddy of all word finders called Catalist.

A website for lovers of the tougher cryptics is run by Derek Harrison in his long-running "The Crossword Centre" at *www.crossword.org.uk*. With numerous links to other relevant sites, it has a lively message board which discusses crosswords from many different sources, albeit tilted towards the tougher crossword.

## 7. Newspaper websites and online solving

Most newspapers now have dedicated crossword websites and have substantially improved them since the last edition of this book. Easy navigability and crossword presentation including a Cheat function to gain individual letters when you're stuck are common. Solving on tablet via these sites is also now much more comfortable and strongly recommended.

**WHY ARE SOME CRYPTICS EASIER THAN OTHERS?**
They may have more anagram clues (perhaps more than half of the total in tabloid crosswords), more hidden clues, more cross-checking in grids, more initial letters cross-checked in grids, no complex constructions, lots of short answers and no obscure ones.

## 8. Blogs (weblogs or daily journals): online cross-word discussion groups

For anyone wanting to know why an answer is what it is, the most helpful daily blogs, contributed by teams of volunteers, are:

For the *Guardian*, *Observer*, *Financial Times*, *Independent* and *Private Eye*:
- Type *Fifteensquared* into a search engine.

For the *Telegraph* and *Sunday Telegraph*:
- Type *Big Dave* into a search engine.

For *The Times* and *The Sunday Times*:
- Type *Times for the Times* into a search engine.

Unlike the others, *The Times* and *The Sunday Times* bloggers are much concerned with their solving times, usually to the nearest second, whilst commenting on what has prevented them from finishing the crossword even faster! You may find this off-putting; nevertheless in line with all other blogs, this site offers a most useful analysis of clues, normally on the day of publication.

**THE CLUE IS IN THE TITLE**
The author Sandy Balfour was so struck with a clue by Rufus in the *Guardian* that he used it as the title of a book on crosswords. The clue is:

*"Pretty girl in crimson rose (8, first letter R, last letter D)."*

The answer is opposite.

## 9. Ximenes book

Don't let it put you off that the next recommendation seems more concerned with barred rather than blocked crosswords. Derrick Macnutt's *Ximenes on the Art of the Crossword*, published first in 1966 and reprinted in 2001, is a book to learn from and enjoy. Derek Harrison (mentioned above) has commented: "This is far more than a treatise, it's thought-provoking and a pleasure to read."

## 10. Setters unmasked

Finally, if you want to discover who lurks behind the curious pseudonyms used by setters, have a look at www.bestforpuzzles.com. They are all there and seem to be kept up to date.

---

**COINCIDENCES**

Enthusiasts spot remarkable happenings in which the same clue appears in different newspapers, sometimes on the same day. Here is one that occurred across continents:

*"It's not a sure thing (8,7)"* (from *The Times*)

About a month earlier, this same clue, word for word was published in *The Hindu*, India's national daily. Lead times would undoubtedly confirm that plagiarism was not the explanation.

The answer is below. Hint: think comma after a.

---

**ANSWER TO SANDWICH CLUE**

Pretty girl in crimson rose (8)

REBELLED – belle in red ("rose" is past tense of "rise" = rebel)

---

**ANSWER TO ADDITIVE CLUE**

It's not a sure thing (8,7)

DEFINITE ARTICLE – definite + article

# 13: Practice Clues by Type

*"In* Brief Encounter *it is Fred Jesson's paradoxical strength that he favours the tortuous lexis of the crossword puzzle over both memory and desire."*

Basil Ransome-Davies, *Spectator* competition to produce a "pseudocrap" review

Before embarking on complete puzzles, you may wish to improve your solving skills by tackling some clues in this section. I suggest this because I have found that learners appreciate the reinforcement of the teaching hitherto by attempting clues grouped by type of clue. They are all sound and sometimes excellent examples of their kind. Many were selected as "Clue of the Week", a long-standing feature of *The Week* magazine in which the best clue from any source is published.

The first five clues in each group offer extra help with first letters of each answer shown after enumeration. Where appropriate, clue type indicators are underlined. Solutions are in the Appendices, from page 179.

---

### ANAGRAM CLUES

1   Shun bad <u>dancing</u> partner (7) H
2   Lady I rather <u>fancy</u> (7) H
3   Greens perhaps <u>misrepresenting</u> Mao Tse-Tung (10) M
4   Looks for brand <u>new</u> UK holiday destination (7,6) N
5   Adhesive tapes <u>come unstuck</u> (5) P
6   Pope with trousers <u>off</u> – that's unthinkable! (12)
7   Break down <u>after moving letters</u> from close pal (8)
8   Guests beginning to get <u>drunk</u> and intimate   (7)
9   Swallow a mouth rinse <u>erroneously</u> (5,6)
10   Where one pays for the other doorbell <u>to be fixed</u> (8)

---

## SANDWICH CLUES

1   It makes us take shelter <u>in</u> centre of Boston? (5) S
2   A half slice of cake <u>in</u> peach trifle (9) B
3   Dope left <u>in</u> bed (4) C
4   Under <u>wraps</u> by choice (6) S
5   Record <u>held by</u> old Delta pilot flying for so long (9) T
6   Shock treatment I <u>received in</u> Harley St in error (9)
7   Terrible rip <u>in</u> chair? I see what you're saying! (3,6)
8   <u>Casually dressed</u> newspaperman stopped by police (6,4)
9   Little girl, one <u>in</u> a hundred (3)
10  Container ship's contents <u>secured by</u> mate (5)

## HOMOPHONE CLUES

1   Rent going up, <u>it's said</u> (4) H
2   Post for a man, <u>so to speak</u> (4) M
3   Praises cricket's HQ <u>on the radio</u> (5) L
4   Naked lady <u>reported</u> in Indian city (3,5) N
5   Flood covering Florence <u>spoken of</u> (8) O
6   <u>Audibly</u> one affected by illness in chest (6)
7   Ways to get to Greek island <u>broadcast</u> (5)
8   <u>Reportedly</u> start race for a pudding (4)
9   Hard stuff in barracks by <u>the sound of it</u> (5)
10  M Easterner in pub, wet <u>one's heard</u> (8)

## TAKEAWAY CLUES

1   <u>Cut</u> price rum (3) O
2   Heresy meets with motion of approval? <u>Not</u> here! (5) S
3   Toilet seat <u>not</u> half wobbly (5) L
4   First <u>off</u> most harsh mountain (7) E
5   WW1 enemy <u>destroying</u> British missile launch site (4) O
6   It's painful <u>extracting</u> penny from sporran (4)
7   Flying Gulf Air, one <u>goes</u> for Economy (6)
8   Trouble brewing over <u>missing</u> murder suspect (6)
9   Doing housework <u>ignoring</u> initial inclination (7)
10  Perhaps stupidly hospital's <u>gone</u> private (6)

## HIDDEN CLUES

1. Peer <u>in</u> Throne Room for King (4) N
2. Pack he'd lead <u>regularly</u> (5) A
3. Brickbats <u>in part</u> of lake (4) F
4. Food item <u>eaten by</u> veggies? (3) E
5. <u>Sample of</u> Nivea's tender skin soap (10) E
6. Sauce requiring <u>a bit of</u> chilli powder (3)
7. <u>Some</u> tarmac cracks in African city (5)
8. Uniform <u>packed and folded</u> by housemaster (4)
9. Fish hate trawler <u>nets</u> (5)
10. Häagen-Dazs <u>retains</u> this secret plan (6)

## REVERSAL CLUES

1. Does perhaps rush <u>around</u> (4) D
2. Bear <u>up</u> – here's a ring (4) H (**down clue**)
3. Put out by <u>mounting</u> objections (4) S (**down clue**)
4. Some privates <u>reversed</u> positions (6) T
5. Type of car to sell <u>back</u> (4) G
6. A medic <u>repelled</u> by appendix (4)
7. Dull poet <u>recalled</u> (4)
8. Huge flans <u>all round</u> – that's the trick! (9)
9. Look in hold <u>on the way back</u> (4)
10. <u>Reversed</u> slump in US fuel (3)

## LETTER SWITCH CLUES

1. Left <u>to replace</u> inner parts of Tchaikovsky score (6) T
2. Do a heart <u>transplant</u> for Tom (5) C
3. What grass is, even <u>for</u> a fool (5) G
4. Highest priest's story – <u>the last shall be first</u> (3) E
5. One taking legal action regrets <u>switching</u> sides (4) S
6. Orderly Helen <u>changing</u> direction in bed (8)
7. Scorn from MP <u>replacing</u> second in contest (8)
8. Dance a little time, last couple <u>swapping places</u> (6)
9. Miss drunken binge, one <u>coming in for</u> a different one (4,2)
10. Like the web? Ladies have <u>a change of</u> heart (5)

## ALL-IN-ONE CLUES

1   Over fifty? <u>Wrong!</u> (5-4) F
2   Setting forth? <u>About</u> right (8) S
3   Join a navy initially as this? (6) S
4   <u>Reverse of</u> fine and cool? (4) N
5   Result of endless spree in which a lot <u>is drunk</u>? (8) B
6   <u>Not normally seen</u> in UK bars! (6)
7   What's displayed on iPhone, extremely large? (5)
8   <u>Fantastic</u> crowd puller? <u>Not half</u>! (5,3)
9   Take part <u>in</u> ruling over nation (6)
10  We will <u>get excited</u> with Ring seats (10)

## DOUBLE DEFINITION CLUES

1   Mad passionate lovers (7) B
2   One photographing a crocodile (7) S
3   Just get the hell out of here! (5) L
4   Herb is a man's name (5) B
5   Honest ie not lying (7) U
6   Don't hit girl! (4)
7   A Greek starter (5)
8   Rhubarb crumble (3)
9   White pawn (4)
10  Press club (4)

## ADDITIVE CLUES

1   Clever person packed underwear (8) B
2   Member of family has information on us (5) G
3   What arrives as August ends? A touch of colour (5) S
4   Small beds for Highlanders (5) S
5   An examination of Chambers (6) A
6   Call at the start before surgery gets busy (3)
7   Maiden cheated? That's by no means rare! (8)
8   Skilful ace, the opposite of gauche (6)
9   Hooded killer from Royal Horse Artillery (4,5)
10  Quiet English girl (3)

## CRYPTIC DEFINITION CLUES

1   Hamburger's first-class? (12) K
2   Pig that flies! (6) G
3   Writer gradually worn down on A4? (6) P
4   Hairdresser's perk? (6,7) F
5   What I must be when small (6) D
6   They have two legs and fly (8)
7   Man United playing away from home (9)
8   Lunch for a cowardly balloonist? (7,2,1,6)
9   A pound of sultanas (5)
10  This cylinder is jammed (5,4)

## NOVELTY CLUES

1   Happen to get 200 in 45 minutes! (5) O
2   Two and six in old money (6,2,5) P
3   Cut off – not dat limb, though! (9) D
4   Program advising accomodation changes? (12) S
5   A swan, deprived of space, sits on this river (5) A
6   Nothing squared is something cubed (3)
7   InterCity? (4)
8   Works for Foreign Office wet? (7)
9   Not having IOU? Aye (9)
10  Sunderland docks (5) (debatable down clue)

### ANONYMOUS OR OTHERWISE?

In 1993 the new editor of the *New York Times* crossword immediately introduced a policy of naming his team of "constructors". Will Shortz decided that setters deserved to be named and besides, he thought correctly that standards would go up as a result. Editor Barbara Hall did the same a little later in the *Sunday Times*. In fact, this policy for cryptic crosswords (with pseudonyms or real names) is common to a majority of newspapers and magazines around the world including those featured in this book. Would solvers like to see setters named in say, the *Daily Mail*, *The Times* and the *Telegraph*? If my students are typical they overwhelmingly would. Could this lead to higher standards? I couldn't possibly comment!

# 14: Practice Puzzles

*"Another day, another cryptic correction – fake clues, I suppose"*
Letter in the *Guardian*

## Introduction
The 24 crosswords starting overleaf are reprinted as they appeared in their named newspapers and magazines. Setters' names, real or pseudonyms, are shown when published. They are in no special order, though the first puzzle is designed to give you a good start. All are chosen as exemplars that should reinforce the principles outlined in earlier chapters.

I think you will agree that the sight of an unfilled grid can be daunting but don't give up at the first hurdle – Mark Goodliffe, a regular and outstanding champion speed solver of *The Times* crossword, has recorded in a blog that he scanned through a dozen or so clues in one of the competition puzzles before finding a single answer. Also remember that there is often an "easy" way in provided by the friendly setter who, after all, does want you to complete and appreciate his or her efforts.

The solutions start on page 187, with clues repeated to avoid unnecessary page-turning. Even if you do not tackle the crosswords, close study of the annotated solutions should be rewarding.

My hope, however, is that you will feel up to the solving challenge and will be surprised how many you can crack with little or no peeking at the solutions.

Please don't worry about time taken and do take a break when stuck – for the greatest pleasure, it shouldn't be a speed contest. In this connection, I once received a letter from an elderly solver saying that my Sunday Mephisto crossword took him nearly the whole week to complete but he liked it that way.

Happy solving!

## Puzzle 1: *The Sun* – Unnamed

**Across**

1 Theatre tutor's old means of transport (10)
8 It does beat vegan food (5)
9 Increases desire, that's swell (7)
10 Pa's about to pull up on the road surface (7)
11 Anchors on open heaths (5)
12 Pull towards a body when Vi a target maybe (9)
15 Shades of colour sound qualities (5)
17 A builder, nearly crazy, can be heard (7)
19 Be a star performing side by side (7)
20 I love stewed fruit (5)
21 Final attempt to endure holiday town (4,6)

**Down**

2 Bulb surprisingly lit up (5)
3 A danger is crushed in Caribbean island (7)
4 Risk total defeat at Wimbledon? (5,8)
5 Tea for fool in the morning (5)
6 Moorhen desperately seeking adrenaline, perhaps (7)
7 Small county where people go to retire? (4)
8 Hear dog in summit (4)
12 Universal soldier (7)
13 A dour disposition you and I found wearying (7)
14 At this point in the rehearsal (4)
15 Quite a knack keeping timber (4)
16 Difficulties with small horses (5)
18 British air ruined wild rose (5)

## Puzzle 2: *Daily Mail* – Unnamed

**Across**

1 Influential condition Elgar noted with pomp (12)
8 Edited and prepared for examination (7)
9 Unsold stock to support record (7)
11 Article men rewrite relating to trade (10)
12 Young animal with one chrysalis (4)
14 Type of swine a danger running around middle of pen (8)
16 Old Spanish change put into plant (6)
17 Grant's regular gun (3)
19 Show off Florida relative (6)
21 Confine remainder at court, keeping Irish back (8)
24 Source of energy at home when he quits (4)
25 Speak once (badly) about good old birthday treat (6,4)
27 Mark grabs money, a lasting power (7)
28 Knot – resolved in daring cut with middle of sword (7)
29 US docker rearranged organs on helm (12)

**Down**

1 Vicar turns up in mixed school with hat on (7)
2 Rarest tuna cooked here? (10)
3 It's more expensive going out modernising (8)
4 Bust smashed by the Parisian's hard to detect (6)
5 Expert runs inside a church
6 Conspire – lines by Unionist put into cipher (7)
7 Fancy farm foie gras? It's thick and creamy (7,5)
10 Promising rain-gauge's working about ten maybe (12)
13 Beat it; English races went ahead in rising gloom (10)
15 Essential part of cereals, crushed (3)
18 Generate broadcast for someone in second decade (8)
20 Head off chaos at a party of green hue (7)
22 I get stuck into translating a Latin language (7)
23 Prominently display Spanish whip (6)
26 Faction's victory over government (4)

## Puzzle 3: *Guardian* – Rufus

### Across

1  Range of company found by MP on a ship (7)
5  Not quite a heavyweight vessel? (7)
9  Bulb lit up, when switched (5)
10 I made case out for specialised schools (5)
11 The constitution should be all the better for them (10)
12 A student is after an alternative exam (4)
14 It may have a good nap on the flight (5,6)
18 Person with two hips? (11)
21 Some harbour dues with which Indians are conversant (4)
22 Break away from the craft (5,5)
25 Exacting examinations involving litmus papers (4,5)
26 One has to be what one is (5)
27 Sending out terminations (7)
28 Getting fed up about midday? (2,5)

### Down

1  A yacht capsized in Old China (6)
2  Striker appears satisfied about everything (6)
3  Ida strips a rampant evergreen (10)
4  Around morning she gets a feeling of guilt (5)
5  Accountant may be after this three-card trick (9)
6  Takes advantage, gaining three points on centre court (4)
7  Footholds on the mount (8)
8  Determined to give poor Rose an instrument (8)
13 Container to list in aircraft manoeuvre (6,4)
15 Sort out that messy collection of stones (9)
16 Precise bill supported by a junior minister (8)
17 It's a blow that has to be faced (8)
19 Girl came in to study the weapon (6)
20 Want to disguise hatred (6)
23 A follower of Ethiopian emperor and a Russian emperor uplifted (5)
24 Heads up to deliver a knockout blow (4)

# Puzzle 4: *Financial Times* – Falcon

## Across

1 Obvious method actors may be seen here in Manhattan (8)

5 Piece of silk? Look at a sample (6)

9 Devious sappers in charge (8)

10 A French child in Germany – it's cruel (2,4)

12 Fortunate, girl receiving king (5)

13 Ivy, maybe, always growing (9)

14 Layout of garrison entered by graduate (6)

16 Dutch scholar, helping to make operas, musicals (7)

19 Each side, initially, on pitch is made up of famous players (3-4)

21 Rock of Gibraltar's third visited by a sailor (6)

23 Talk in nightclub? Sure, when drunk (9)

25 What a bishop may wear in a joint (5)

26 New weapon, restricted (6)

27 Ankle was broken in ballet (4,4)

28 Written message from landlord's in character (6)

29 One-time collier penning article for paper? (8)

## Down

1 Check back of veil worn by groom's partner (6)

2 The traditional type from Harrow, for example (3,6)

3 Dry It in cocktail is nasty (5)

4 A new European coin embodying one that's very old (7)

6 Saw single storm-tossed schooner, say (9)

7 Junk food (5)

8 Pleasure-seeker, male lecturer, is sort of square (8)

11 Lake shimmered somewhat (4)

15 Device that marks time – encountered no more, strangely (9)

17 Early form of transport (4,5)

18 Lie about filming a naughty nude in colour (3,2,3)

20 Seldom seen underdone (4)

21 Polish insects get larger (7)

22 Nothing in measuring device can show a shooting star (6)

24 Fish in foreign parts (5)

25 Note that goes up or down (5)

## Puzzle 5: *Daily Telegraph* – Unnamed

**Across**

1 Skill fixing fence, if icy (10)
6 Bound to leave (4)
9 Vehicles, vehicles – about time! (5)
10 Select Poe works to shorten (9)
12 Old bishop and minister in study (7)
13 Rushed for instance towards the West's diversity (5)
15 Agitated conductor leading band's climax (7)
17 Former lover suggested getting bare (7)
19 Country retreat with distinguishing characteristic (7)
21 Hearing sounds back, son must be captivated (7)
22 Model of car and every train (5)
24 Business skill returned: very loudly in charge (7)
27 Keeping in power involved keeping quiet (9)
28 Say nothing in sin (5)
29 Holy man, the old thing that's painful to see around (4)
30 Fired up, 50 per cent of encounters were angry (10)

**Down**

1 Branch of sweet chestnut's cut (4)
2 Catch up after pro got left behind (9)
3 Charges people from the Highlands leading southern moves? (5)
4 Went in hospital department before daughter (7)
5 Company suggest leaving a place of learning (7)
7 Recognised kind of wine regularly taken out (5)
8 Putting on an act before start of theatrical finale (10)
11 What person in the Navy could want rubbish on board ship? (7)
14 Customs raid – it's not unusual (10)
16 Mad king wielding the whip (7)
18 Some tailors initially longing to finish this? (9)
20 Thick stews in French cuisine, as they say in Paris (7)
21 Head cleaner has mop bent over (7)
23 Refusal to tuck into any bug (5)
25 Female continually creating state of excitement (5)
26 Heroic exploit, whichever way you look at it (4)

## Puzzle 6: *Oxford Times* – Colin Dexter

**Across**

1 Joint cover – not comprehensive though (9)
6 Party Mr Heath loved excessively (5)
9 Sweet Jane? Name first with Tarzan (7)
10 Rein? Initially, no colt could be without it (7)
11 Plants do, in Channel Islands (5)
12 Job in which you could make lots of brass (9)
13 Northampton Town FC are rubbish! (8)
15 One's weak – one to get a PM cross? (4)
19 Spirit shown by Mandela (Nelson) (4)
20 Bane, this, if much drunk (8)
23 Posh crockery – present for the old Dutch (9)
24 Spy one shark here, maybe? (5)
26 Half-bike whizzed with pace around part of Delhi? (7)
27 They flutter etc. – mostly timid (7)
28 Sort of mush to bed Umbelliferae at first (5)
29 Quietly in love with rest? The outcome, perhaps (9)

**Down**

1 Bio-system peddled, it's said, in Health Shop (4,5)
2 Like column in a Palladio niche? (5)
3 Quack's shouldering responsibility, if it's broken (8)
4 How to be cleverer? O, must work with skill (8)
5 Divine Power from the Catechism (6)
6 Bradman's famous duck (6)
7 It's shocking to embrace wrongdoing: that's him though, to a "T" (9)
8 Drink in Denmark is automatically controlled (5)
14 Twist made bold about second helping of meat? This stopped that (9)
16 Bush-whackers criticize the new one? (9)
17 Tease Ben cruelly, but one is not ticked off (8)
18 With which best idea is to get treatment (8)
21 A lot of hay (6)
22 If one's shooting, aim for the panda! (6)
23 In the main, such a charge is damaging (5)
25 Feature surrounding one always at disco (5)

## Puzzle 7: *The Oldie* – Antico

Each of six clues consists of definitions of two words of different lengths. In each case, one of the words, which is the answer to be entered in the grid, is created when a letter 20 the other word. The letters in question, in clue order, spell 10. The words of 10 20 were written by a person whose name appears in the top and bottom rows. Numbers in brackets refer to lengths of grid entries.

**Across**

7 Discover doctor in control (6)
8 Commemoration returning each year, in essence, after end of parade (7)
11 Top combination in university assignment (9)
12 Searches for favourite places (5)
13 Time yet to be abandoning boundaries with new change of policy (1-4)
15 Purity corrupted once inside pub before church (9)
17 Negative response by letter, out of order, not using right item of stationery (7)
19 Contemporary work, one about filling time left (7)
21 Puss stopped by road beside fit place for nap? (4,5)
23 Policeman taking a trail back (5)
24 Tap side of cut gem (5)
26 Be drawn, endlessly critical, into scrape (9)
28 Price put up for daub (7)
29 Gives out pieces of absorbent paper (6)

**Down**

1 Clear hesitation with magistrate around (4)
2 Serious, first off, about king (6)
3 One after pleasure in hold-up plugged by crime boss (8)
4 Groom left at end of meal? (6)
5 Near agreement, raised drink at bedtime (8)
6 Story by vagrant with odd bits cut out (4)
9 Son admitted to loathing hurry (5)
14 Thorough grumble (5)
16 Some macaroni certainly more agreeable (5)
18 Line on bird penned by poet lacking finish and freedom (8)
19 Tact I managed, skirting edge of subject (8)
21 Hits, latest in music, very loud in America (5)
22 Incompetent producer of taps? (6)
23 Good to get over anger, catching second salmon (6)
25 Collected part of engine broken by learner (4)
27 Declare answer and upset vicar (4)

## Puzzle 8: *Sunday Times* – Tim Moorey

**Across**

1 Courage not on tap – poor deliveries (2,5)
5 F Field and B Silver in rundown hotel (7)
9 One remains to occupy post in water plant (5,4)
10 Learner inside just showing style (5)
11 Island holiday (6)
12 Private parking near New Orleans (8)
14 Fruit celebrity requests one's overlooked (4,6)
16 Mug returned and put down (4)
18 Newlywed not good in kitchen perhaps (4)
19 Laughing a lot as one may be on leaving theatre (2,8)
22 After rough handling Roget did get worn out (3-5)
23 William gets love? A lot if like this! (5-1)
26 Basket producer there is only backed in part (5)
27 Get garage rebuilt and you may need this (9)
28 Bums are held back in clothes (7)
29 I defy you to give boozer present (2,5)

**Down**

1 Book for anaesthetists? (7)
2 Mugs from a county (5)
3 City girl hanging around star (3,5)
4 Feeling of humiliation mostly false (4)
5 Plates can be represented as the feet around Bow in London (5,5)
6 Short on top, egotistical and mischievous (6)
7 Condition of lingerie at the laundry! (9)
8 Uniform line by journalist confused (7)
13 Cadge a lot in bathroom containers (6,4)
15 Rogue dealing so close to a bank? (9)
17 Second missile is urgent (8)
18 Endure southern resort mentioned? Unacceptable (4,3)
20 Language being taken up? Nothing in it (7)
21 This is evidently the first and last in saloon cars (6)
24 Let pound drop a bit (5)
25 Potential birdies, maybe eagles (4)

## Puzzle 9: *Observer* – Everyman

### Across

1 See vine tangled with herb (8)
5 Abandon thread (6)
9 Covered past life initially with relief (8)
10 Is painful technique used in texting? (6)
12 Environmentalist's signal to proceed (5)
14 Custom immune to criticism from airman blushing aboard boat (6,3)
15 Propose measure before social gathering for indoor game (5,8)
17 Certainly sense hot excitement of bout, duo receiving cheers (7,1,5)
21 Resistance in territory by soldier, cold and calculated (9)
22 Greek character absorbed by argument he tackled (5)
23 License book in revolutionary electronic way (6)
24 Unlucky one, round in valley, in retreat (3-5)
26 Thirsty to grab attention? Not interesting (6)
27 Linguistic unit in translation of sly label (8)

### Down

1 Stretch, with energy left, operating barrier (8)
2 Struggle with unfinished scene (3)
3 Quiet because occupied by French article (7)
4 Artist captures nobody's heart? Harsh (12)
6 Paint moderate area (7)
7 Curtail urge to reform land management (11)
8 Deny any connection with inspector, planted (6)
11 English clubs still followed by supporter very happily (12)
13 Inclination, changing gear, to cut extra hard work (5,6)
16 Trio, not half oppressed by burden, cross (8)
18 Gossip time after time going into story? Right (7)
19 Responsible university scientist finally separating new fluid (7)
20 Move up when around goal (6)
25 Clumsy boat yet to capsize (3)

## Puzzle 10: *The Week* – Tim Moorey

Italicized clues are fanciful definitions from BBC Radio 4's "I'm Sorry I Haven't a Clue" as collected in the Uxbridge English Dictionary. More normal definitions (in random order) are: DANCE, PROCLAIM, MOANS, OUTLINE, DIE, COMBINE, VEGETABLE, ARTIFICE, SEATING, CAFETERIA, A TV AID and 2 DRINKS.

### Across

1 *What Australians make wine from* (6)
4 Service veteran manipulated figures (8)
10 *Traffic jam* (7)
11 *Concorde* (7)
12 Euphoric greeting heard (4)
13 Croatian resort calls for key holders (5,5)
15 *Toast by the Queen* (6)
16 *Woman from Finland* (7)
20 *To stop stopping* (7)
21 Juliet say, mostly getting highly addictive drug (6)
24 Nurses seen around coral island with religious leaders (10)
26 Public protest in Delaware and Missouri (4)
28 *Nonsense spoken by taxi-drivers* (7)
29 *One who has reached the age of consent* (7)
30 Unnecessary sharp pointers succeeded initially (8)
31 *Someone who is coughed upon* (6)

### Down

1 Number missing, chap rings out for computer images (8)
2 *Answer to question: Where's t' coal?* (9)
3 Engrave two thirds of rough drawing (4)
5 *Cockney dentures* (8)
6 Badly depressed about university and get displaced (10)
7 Elderly relative consumes one cereal (5)
8 Sweet pastry one's seen in bowl (6)
9 Times casual worker looking down on one (5)
14 Wide-ranging discussion costing nothing? (4-3-3)
17 A softened composition? No good for one such (5-4)
18 What's added at the end changes liturgical books (8)
19 *28 grams* (8)
22 *Tintin's partner* (3-3)
23 Sun journalist in roughly built hut (5)
25 Blame invalid for a slow walk (5)
27 Data from rain-forest (4)

## Puzzle 11: *Sunday Telegraph* – Unnamed

### Across

1 Kind of ball fashioned around square, oddly (10)
6 Appear in place of bishop, taking mass (4)
9 HQ for force in Waterloo, say (7)
10 Poke fun at a politician in flier (7)
12 Attractive urgent coverage for legal support team (13)
14 Surfing, maybe at equator (6)
15 PC, for example, frantically cut rope binding maiden (8)
17 Former partner having case for enforcement of payment (8)
19 In war, can accept things being kept secret (6)
22 Group of swimmers before the race upset instructor (13)
24 Academic penning papers is tiresome (5,2)
25 Clubs make certain statement attributing blame (7)
26 Home for nocturnal creature fixed ahead of time (4)
27 Have second thoughts about condition covering European disadvantages (10)

### Down

1 Get engaged repeatedly in schemes Holmes hatched (4)
2 It's used for opening act in theatre (7)
3 Global organisation badly tainted within alliances (6,7)
4 Organised party membership, initially unsystematic (6)
5 Study about soul I misrepresented in error (8)
7 I'll feature prominently in his speech (7)
8 Like those in charge, chap set over African country shifting left (10)
11 Doesn't understand I'm upset, perhaps wrongly, over aims (13)
13 Serious type, in this way, also embracing monarch (10)
16 Carry on once unit is given new order (8)
18 Put the "A" in art, essentially (2,5)
20 On the rocks, possibly needing silver bullet (7)
21 Cut short awkward old cowboy (6)
23 It sounds like sweetheart does, for instance (4)

## Puzzle 12: *Independent on Sunday* – Hoskins

**Across**

1 Mess that an angler might have had a hand in? (3,2,5)

6 You could say I am good about clothes (4)

10 A brief dram plus Bud – that's living (7)

11 Nasty complaint impeding cavity? Bend over! (7)

12 Did this, being annoyed about wife (5)

13 Amazed to see One Direction having fight (9)

14 Get out of it, perhaps with individual on Bass (6)

16 Slips away from area and sleeps around (7)

18 Time Her Maj should enter a service sober (7)

21 Incidents in the 100 and 200 metres? (6)

24 I'd neither gone off or was left (9)

25 In flagrante, but half-upset (cold room) (5)

26 Half-pint of cider taken regularly after whisky? (7)

27 Beast always chasing after flushed duke (3,4)

28 Having changed top, bother to work out? (4)

29 Cook did entrées, then pounded the meat? (10)

**Down**

1 Rough business heading waste disposal unit? (6)

2 I'm soon dancing on E and awfully smelly (7)

3 Stitch up celebrity cut by Republican leader (5)

4 Work and work with energy on speed (7)

5 Teach me to fly a chopper in the jungle? (7)

7 Ways a love goddess will inspire ecstasy (7)

8 Salty bishop cut twice is full of anguish (8)

9 Hint of a strangler in Danny Dyer's face (4,5)

15 Extra charge to put May in the good PM category? (8)

17 What completes Liam of Oasis: wrestling dons? (8)

19 German building kitsch, loss-making houses (7)

20 Intense, but unopened message about Hoskins (7)

21 Stop, you ruddy bore (7)

22 Are they a bit higher than belly laughs? (7)

23 So lacking in love, my editor bought drugs (6)

25 Summer days in embrace of a European Romeo (5)

## Puzzle 13: *The Times* – Unnamed

**Across**

1  Scraps in a shower after match (8)
6  Got staff back in case of blockage (6)
9  Snow still coming from the east (4)
10 Plunder left misery (10)
11 Leaves flight with first team (5,5)
13 After second-half switch, many confused (4)
14 Tube list for commuting displayed translation (8)
16 Rather silly how the Queen is represented (6)
18 Rest on slopes after a set-back (6)
20 American finding room to work in between areas a lot reduced (8)
22 Who might get caught for parking in area for vegetables? (4)
24 Key for a disappointed officer? (1-4,5)
26 Amphibian say, lacking stern and seen in the sea near Calais (10)
28 Periods of time mostly put out of one's mind (4)
29 Curse flipping metal having a screw loose (4,2)
30 Possible advice from Walton for this musical accompaniment? (8)

**Down**

2  Wanting introductions, veiled and dowdy woman to use a superior club? (9)
3  Shabby place bound to be shown in correspondence (7)
4  Back of court seat originally providing cover for a seed (5)
5  Response ministers get in artificial language (3)
6  Bare all in dancing? I wouldn't do that! (9)
7  Crown singer Fitzgerald a star (7)
8  Customs needing extra staff initially (5)
12 Face rocks in unfavourable part of Everest? (3,4)
15 Rent wrong around Californian valley meeting resistance (4,5)
17 Complex lecture supporting European party (9)
19 Keep belting runs and leave coach behind (7)
21 Not a strong attorney in the Spanish way (7)
23 Fix up with a climber (5)
25 Starts tea for an audience with appropriate vessels (5)
27 Quack comes from duck confined by US district (3)

## Puzzle 14: *The Times Quick Cryptic* – Dazzler

**Across**

1 In Australia a capital idea and deal that's extraordinary (8)

5 Dessert made by wife with it (4)

8 Fellow boxing minute title-holder (5)

9 Effectiveness of company shown by data extremely clearly (7)

11 Feel airport needs changing to grow rapidly (11)

13 US author to judge verse (6)

14 Complete current book and part of play (6)

17 Boy accompanying Queen twice is a Casanova (11)

20 Famous authoress with no name on grave (7)

21 Group of revolutionary activists with duke in charge (5)

22 American is a jerk (4)

23 Traveller always recalled carrying one spare (8)

**Down**

1 Knowing military music hasn't started (4)

2 Model partner once generous (7)

3 Take illegally? Right (11)

4 Nothing that is dear (6)

6 Dye hard girl picked up (5)

7 Nasty MEP fiddled allowances (8)

10 Market trader perhaps is inexperienced and rather vulgar, we hear (11)

12 Curate finally happy in restored church festival (8)

15 Cross written at bottom of a contract (7)

16 Stick lands regularly at this spot (6)

18 Playwright identified by some lines bitterly upset (5)

19 Garden party making fortune reportedly (4)

## Puzzle 15: *The Times Quick Cryptic* – Joker

**Across**

1  Severely criticise left for understanding (7)
5  Wrong a young lady (5)
8  Nearly all rib coach for filter on entry to the cup (3-8)
10 Region of Far East (4)
11 Conservative's initial whipping leads to arguing (8)
12 Recent milky espresso needs sugar, ultimately (6)
14 Who deals with ship's hold or deck when working (6)
16 Train too awkward for turning round (8)
18 Beginning to produce beer with little colour (4)
20 One who asked for more fruit takes right new treatment (6,5)
22 Process of colouring material without energy is failing (5)
23 Written as poetry upside down (7)

**Down**

2  Change of flag that's not the first (5)
3  Game bird losing head to horrible farm worker (7)
4  What one doesn't like to be discovered in trattoria? (3)
6  Artist – one from Bavarian capital (5)
7  Unusual stone found on top of a series of hills (7)
9  A group on leave (7)
11 Wow! Lovely ornamental moulding (7)
13 A game with generally hollow defence (7)
15 Fancy limit being put on staple food (7)
17 Foreign sci-fi film (5)
19 Sacred water lily louts destroyed (5)
21 One hundred mph – never going over (3)

## Puzzle 16: *The Times Quick Cryptic* – Orpheus

**Across**

1 Church member entertaining a top boxer, perhaps (5)

4 Report of district that's more breezy (6)

9 Italian physicist's brief month on island? (7)

10 Old railwaymen given points to look after (5)

11 Uproar in first half of meal (3)

12 Her deli's output is greatly enjoyed (8)

15 Obliging, acting as a landlord? (13)

17 Tear delicate fabric, meeting cost (8)

18 Bachelor originally attending tennis club (3)

20 Old England cricketer's elegance of manner? (5)

22 One with no illusions about a register (7)

23 Remove obstruction in river (6)

24 Unusually regal composer (5)

**Down**

1 Entertainer's scam involving TV, press etc (8)

2 In favour of wearing a new pinafore? (5)

3 Broadcast made by expert with very little weight (9)

5 Pub that's popular: Nag's Head (3)

6 Like Ben-Gurion, head off British prime minister (7)

7 Genuine-sounding Scottish dance (4)

8 Rich person's factory, one on Yorkshire river (11)

13 Unoriginal friend's impasse in chess (9)

14 Rabble-rouser finally appearing at a riot, unhappily (8)

16 French painter left to support tea girl (7)

18 Old crooner accepts pound for flashy jewellery (5)

19 A good press chief much advanced in years (4)

21 Tailed amphibian familiar at first in sci-fi film (3)

## Puzzle 17: *The Times Quick Cryptic* – Grumpy

**Across**

1 Tough guys breaking ribs? Sure! (8)
5 Like one with a large land-mass (4)
9 Queen follows favourite saint (5)
10 A word we hear in a German accent? So it's alleged (7)
11 Cooler that is cold inside (3)
12 Proposed name I don't change (9)
13 I'm taken aback by anger? That's an illusion (6)
15 Sibling ignoring the second disturbance (6)
17 Lorna's family has least amount of data to contribute (2,4,3)
19 Sprite seen in hotel foyer (3)
20 Tie up an awkward flower (7)
21 Confused when sailing? (2,3)
22 Mormon's end beside salt lake (4)
23 Begin to understand material one doesn't finish (6,2)

**Down**

1 Initiation that's suitable is in British Museum (7)
2 Family member doesn't start to let loose (5)
3 Jump on places for putting veg (6,6)
4 Province in actual centre of Germany (5)
6 Withdraw from minor injury (7)
7 Extra snake almost died (5)
8 Simple dish – not as snob ate in mess (5,2,5)
14 Cock Robin initially waving to Rose (7)
16 Hold back from the chorus (7)
17 Extremely desirable drug store (5)
18 Encouraging word for Charlie's predecessor (5)
19 Uncommon sense in a German city (5)

## Puzzle 18: *The Times Quick Cryptic* – Marty

**Across**

1 Alec stands waving something on the beach (10)
8 Offer comfort to Tory only (7)
9 Some backing from fair American girl (5)
10 Jolly experience with LSD? (4)
11 Rudely jeer any English novel (4,4)
13 Expelled school inspectorate, making one change (6)
14 Entices office workers? About time (6)
17 Raw treat prepared for amphibious rodent (5,3)
19 Wonderful going round foremost of night spots (4)
21 Does walk, say, regularly in Japanese city (5)
22 Minor quarrel to have in Cheltenham? (3,4)
23 Music hall song, unspecific request to golf caddie? (3,3,4)

**Down**

2 Article completes the undoing of relatives (7)
3 Party, alternatively, providing means of escape? (4)
4 Primate's name secretary recalled (6)
5 Be visibly embarrassed after little boy beamed (8)
6 Nobleman years ahead of his time? (5)
7 Maybe Chinese food at the back (3,7)
8 Protective material, designed to cool, won't (6,4)
12 To prepare vintage, tread year's contents (3,5)
15 Picture army officer with old musical instrument (7)
16 Young lady distributed medals (6)
18 Jewelled headdress: it elevated a painter (5)
20 Garment starts off small and rarely increases (4)

## Puzzle 19: *The Times Quick Cryptic* – Tracy

### Across

1 Vessel behind heading for small Channel island (4)
3 Pair watch, perhaps, for unfaithful partner (3-5)
9 First half of song softly managed by old singer (7)
10 Invalidate yearbook, removing second article (5)
11 Turn out to be point ahead (3,2)
12 Good access for aristocracy (6)
14 Hate it, a late TV broadcast, but take no further action (5,2,2,4)
17 Basic piano installed in flat (6)
19 Come back again about aggressive dog (5)
22 Crime rendering rector powerless? (5)
23 First sign (7)
24 Dance enthusiast circling with energy (8)
25 Supporting Democrat, unelected President (4)

### Down

1 Kind, like a senior nurse? (8)
2 Quick attack trapping leader of pack (5)
4 Daydreaming in court, appearing before large assembly (13)
5 Do exercises in school (5)
6 Rally rounding on head of state (7)
7 Function of list, reportedly (4)
8 Specimen provided by son, more than enough (6)
13 Set off, went out in front, surprised (8)
15 Skilled worker from Hobart is a natural (7)
16 Go home and go to bed (4,2)
18 Herbivore filling saucepan, daily (5)
20 Company about to broadcast in capital (5)
21 Homeless child would appear in front, first of all (4)

## Puzzle 20: *The Times Quick Cryptic* – Howzat

### Across

4 Irregular dates happily in the end becoming a regular one? (6)

7 Portrait of Somalian vandalised (4,4)

8 Countless millions taken by milk producer rejected (6)

9 Intimate change and say nothing (5,3)

10 Mean singing voice heard (4)

12 Pork cut in box served with processed brie (5,3)

15 Quiet craftsman is prejudiced (8)

18 Quits flat (4)

20 Sergeant in mess put out of favour (8)

22 Sounding cold, it's hot (6)

23 Good on imposing French city! (8)

24 Cockney wife having lost capital, is after credit support (6)

### Down

1 Dimwit who is also sweet (4)

2 Sort of artist in a way associated with flags (8)

3 US soldier hires out padded jackets (6)

4 Greek island associated with a savoury snack (6)

5 Rehearsals in part for organs (4)

6 Due date that's not welcomed by caller? (8)

11 Secure a time with TV presenter (2,6)

13 Highest point almost for pulse (3)

14 One way of getting to the top in say, Washington (8)

16 Seasonal transport is murder, one's heard (6)

17 Madman from northern state (6)

19 Scheduled time for opening (4)

21 Misses prodigal son? Not entirely (4)

## Puzzle 21: *The Times Quick Cryptic* – Teazel

**Across**

1 Selecting a ballad that's cheap (5,3,1,4)
8 Underground gets new head, consciously old-fashioned (5)
9 Amused mark of approval came first (7)
10 Kitchen utensil, I hear, is larger (7)
11 Track down a tiny quantity (5)
13 Intended recipient of notice sees red, being replaced (9)
17 Relatives found in usual places, commonly (5)
19 Travelled zigzag courses as told, an imposition on driver (4,3)
20 Unable to sail in a grand circle (7)
22 Body recently demoted from place ordered out (5)
23 Mad not to be playing with nursery horse? (3,4,6)

**Down**

1 Say, a cloth picked up in motor home (6)
2 Largely at sea (2,3,4)
3 Exulted, told age was wrong (7)
4 Subeditor here corrected "British Isles" (5,8)
5 A Hibernian course (5)
6 First off, burn fuel (3)
7 Wander about to obtain device (6)
12 Very afraid weak crust has collapsed (9)
14 Hair product, counterfeit and low quality, not finished (7)
15 Tries a drop in house (3,1,2)
16 Area of Somerset, no longer low, with river? (6)
18 Disdain incentive, finally stubborn (5)
21 Concerned with following man on the pitch (3)

# Puzzle 22: *The Times Quick Cryptic* – Flamande

## Across

1  Preserves link, recruiting English spy (5,4)
6  Old boy repulsed by a snake (3)
8  Like a boy left with his dad, unusually (7)
9  Show off volume by family member (5)
10 Angelic, sober sort, easy to spot (12)
12 Pamper group on Greek island (6)
13 Social occasions welcomed by proud ancestors (6)
16 Such perfect vision two decades into this century? (6-6)
19 One doesn't like shifting earth (5)
20 Send society girl back, now it's late evening? (7)
22 Nothing in mill, after removal of odd components (3)
23 Insignificant man on board one evening after work? (9)

## Down

1  Girl unwell after onset of jaundice (4)
2  Finish up interrupting church service? That's insane (7)
3  Originally, six kilometres impossible for runner in winter (3)
4  Mostly, one casual worker is available (2,4)
5  Destroy borders of Delaware and Virginia, say (9)
6  Obscure book? This description might help (5)
7  Recasts failing performer (7)
11 Defeat leader of hecklers in public spat (9)
12 Understand how to become popular (5,2)
14 Press item causing offence (7)
15 Secure small item of furniture (6)
17 Acclaim former tax reduced by one pound (5)
18 Socialists abandoned side (4)
21 Lecturer seen in Oxford, once (3)

## Puzzle 23: *The Times Quick Cryptic* – Hawthorn

**Across**

1   Some heavy rain for us after low pressure (8)
5   Spoils of war personified (4)
8   Drink large rum (5)
9   M Escher, perplexing creator of intricate designs? (7)
11  Vehicle parked in Pennsylvania (3)
12  Rotten season for the Cubs? (9)
13  Word for scoundrel to be announced in newspaper (6)
15  Adhesive binding agent: revolutionary building material (6)
18  Destroyed nicotine, protecting hearts at risk (2,4,3)
19  Stick man (3)
20  Grandma getting into Dickens, a rewarding discovery (7)
21  Nation state rejecting North America (5)
22  Thanks company for Mexican snack (4)
23  Plant fake diamond? (8)

**Down**

1   Take back hated present (7)
2   Cart succeeded at transporting silver (5)
3   Prepared point for ear piercing (11)
4   Use fan on the blink? That's risky (6)
6   Tramp is moving around smelly places? (7)
7   Shoulder manoeuvre seen in Welsh rugby (5)
10  Satisfactory compromise: one likely to lift spirits? (5,6)
14  Hugely powerful wrench in attic (7)
16  Cosmetic treatment getting daughter and dad covered in dirt (7)
17  Hard day Inland Revenue turned up for capital (6)
18  Annual circulation in relation to the Sun? (5)
19  Travelled over for traditional US event (5)

## Puzzle 24: *The Times Quick Cryptic* – Hurley

**Across**

1 In Caracas sat awaiting ice cream (7)
5 Exchange involving Mike's waterlogged area (5)
8 Defective seascapes clue? These might give way out (6,7)
9 Complicated time: old invader departs (7)
10 Speaker's arguments for ordinary writing (5)
11 Succeeded at first with aloof manner in island (6)
13 Somewhat retro stereotyped work list (6)
15 Make changes in plug fitting (5)
16 Agile learner lives a bit (7)
19 Well-known type of room for water board? (6,7)
20 Left-winger returning with English cake (5)
21 Difficult situation of throaty Sue, pasty regularly (3,4)

**Down**

1 Talk about energy fraud (5)
2 Back Companion of Honour over warning colour in House of Lords perhaps (6,7)
3 Dad upset over friend's dismay (5)
4 Are gripping rascal in shopping precinct (6)
5 Soapy liquid not what it seems, poor, ultimately lacking (7)
6 The cartoonist upset, having little advance warning (2,5,6)
7 Pioneering chemist super at broadcast (7)
11 Refuse to leave street? Indeed, sulk forgetting nothing (4,3)
12 Large upper room with Eastern ornamental pattern (7)
14 Roughly hustle investigator (6)
17 Pole's second attempt to win (5)
18 Country for example you passed through initially (5)

# 15: Difficulty Ranking in Newspapers

*"I wish he would explain his explanation."*
Lord Byron, Don Juan

At the end of my workshops, I give suggestions as to which nationally available blocked puzzles students might try after the course, taking account of solving difficulty and pleasure. It's a list that hasn't changed much for several years. Of course, assessment of difficulty levels varies between assessors but this is mine.

The **starred bands** below are what I perceive to be the approximate order of their difficulty. Crosswords within each group are also in increasing levels of difficulty, though this is even more subjective.

Many of these puzzles are available online, some of them free or requiring a small payment.

## \* DAILY MIRROR, DAILY STAR, THE SUN AND THEIR WEEKEND SISTERS

Ximenean principles are sometimes stretched in this group; they have considerably more anagrams and hidden clues than others. Their answer words are straightforward; literary, art and musical references are few. Grids may have fewer than average blocked squares, increasing cross-checking possibilities and some answers may be fully "checked", such that solvers can find an answer appearing without having solved the clue. Some of these crosswords have two sets of clues (cryptic and non-cryptic) for the same grid, a feature that's really valued by complete beginners.

## \*\* DAILY MAIL, MAIL ON SUNDAY, DAILY EXPRESS, SUNDAY EXPRESS

These all follow Ximenean principles to a large extent and have a large loyal and satisfied solvership.

*** **TIMES QUICK CRYPTIC, DAILY TELEGRAPH**
For those solving Quick crosswords currently, these two are excellent in helping a transition to cryptics.

**** **OBSERVER EVERYMAN, SUNDAY TELEGRAPH, FINANCIAL TIMES, THE OLDIE GENIUS, THE WEEK, THE SUNDAY TIMES, INDEPENDENT AND THE I NEWSPAPER, INDEPENDENT ON SUNDAY, PRIVATE EYE**
This large group is the one in which difficulty level varies the most. Most of them will include clues with topical references. One or two lesser-known words may well be included and there can be some stretching of definitional meanings. Note that the *Independent* newspapers, *Financial Times* and *Sunday Times* have more than one setter which inevitably leads to more variability, but also more loyalty to individual setters. Apart from the *Observer* and the *Sunday Telegraph*, all these publications name their setters, using pseudonyms or real names.

***** **TIMES, GUARDIAN, DAILY TELEGRAPH TOUGHIE**
These three also have a panel of setters, named in the Toughie and *Guardian* but not in *The Times*. Day-by-day difficulty levels can vary considerably, sometimes being close to the three star group, other days a long way from that. A *Guardian* poll showed that solvers are happy with this, most voting for an occasional very tough challenge and that is probably true for *Times* solvers. The more complex constructions referred to in Chapter 9 may make the occasional appearance in both of these two puzzles.

The *Guardian* crossword has a number of setters whose clues are further away from Ximenes than any other daily newspaper. That's not to pass judgment on quality or enjoyment – it is to say that potential solvers following this book will find they need to think laterally and more deeply than for the other crosswords. However, familiarity with each setter's tricks does of course help considerably. The *Guardian*'s Araucaria, who died in November 2013, was in a special category of his own as being both proudly non-Ximenean and much loved, especially for his original themes and long anagrams. He is also the only setter so far to have received the MBE and to have made an appearance on *Desert Island Discs*. His puzzles are still available in book form and online.

What people want in addition are recommendations for those that might give extra pleasure and are at the easiest end of the solving range in their newspapers.

Not including my own puzzles and recognising that this is highly subjective, I recommend this elite group, based not only on workshop participant feedback but also on the ultimate test of which setters cause me to buy the newspaper in question:

**SETTERS**
Appearing regularly having a single setter:
*Observer* Everyman, *Sunday Telegraph*, *The Oldie Genius*, *Private Eye* Cyclops (not for sensitive souls!)

Appearing under pseudonyms:
*Guardian* Arachne, Brendan, Pasquale, Picaroon; Telegraph Toughie: Messinae; Independent: eXternal, Dac
Times Quick Cryptic – all setters recommended

Not only do these conform fully to the teaching outlined in this book, they usually offer smooth surface meanings and ingenious wordplay. For those wanting themes (and I'm aware that some solvers do not), the *Oldie* is always themed with a preamble. The Brendan puzzles are often themed, albeit that the theme may not be apparent until the end. Incidentally, for anyone wondering what a themed puzzle is, there are two in this book (Puzzles 7 and 10).

In a category of its own, with regularly brilliant puzzles, is *The Times* including its weekend Jumbo crossword, though I hesitate to make a specific regular daily recommendation as difficulty levels vary and its many setters are unnamed.

## WHICH CROSSWORD BOOK NEXT?

For readers wanting lots more information on crossword setting, editing and many other aspects, especially on advanced cryptics such as Azed in the *Observer* and Mephisto in the *Sunday Times*, the book to go for is *Chambers Crossword Manual* by Don Manley.

For readers who want more practice on the down-to-earth cryptics in this book, I strongly recommend any of the *Times Quick Cryptic Crossword* books (NB not the *Times Quick Crossword* books). Each contains 100 of the puzzles originally published in Times2. They have reduced grids (13 by 13) and, as already stated, reduced difficulty from that of the perhaps daunting main *Times* crossword, thus suiting those with limited time and encouraging people to take their first steps in cryptics.


## THE MOST PROLIFIC CROSSWORD SETTER?

Now retired, Roger Squires set nearly 75,000 puzzles and over 2 million clues for the *Telegraph, Guardian* and others.

Marc Breman, setting anonymously for the likes of *Daily Mirror* and *Express*, is another prolific setter. His profile was boosted by dubbing one puzzle as the world's hardest that would take two years to complete. Unfortunately, this claim was disproved when at least one solver cracked it in under two hours!


## TOP TIP – INDIRECT ABBREVIATIONS

Most of the abbreviations opposite are "direct" eg bishop = B. However, you are likely to find some of an "indirect" nature eg "medic = doctor DR, MB or MO and "business or firm" = company = CO.


## TOP TIP – DOUBLED ABBREVIATIONS

Occasionally you may need to "think plural abbreviation" if you're stuck with, say, "goods", "dates" and even "smalls". These could stand for GG, DD and SS.

# PART 4

# APPENDICES

*"How clean is your house? Meet the crossword fanatic who has not cleaned her flat for 24 years."*
Channel 4 TV Listings

## 1. List of Abbreviations

This list includes the most common crossword abbreviations and all of those used in this book's clues and puzzles. To assist solvers, it is arranged in order of the abbreviated word rather than the abbreviation itself.

| | | | | | |
|---|---|---|---|---|---|
| about | CA, RE | cold | C | female | F |
| ace | A | companion | CH | fifty | L |
| adult | A | company | CO | fine | F |
| airman | AC | Conservative | C | first person | I |
| Ambassador | HE | constant | C | following | F |
| American | US | copper | CU | force | F |
| answer | A | court | CT | former | EX |
| artist | RA | credit | CR | forte | F |
| attorney | DA | | | | |
| | | date | D | gallons | G |
| | | daughter | D | good | G |
| bass | B | day | D | government | G |
| bill | AC | Democrat | D | graduate | MA, BA |
| bishop | B | departs | D | | |
| black | B | diamonds | D | grand | G |
| book | B | died | D | gunners | RA |
| born | B | doctor | DR | | |
| bowled | B | Duke | D | hard | H |
| breadth | B | | | hearts | H |
| British | B | East(ern) | E | height | H |
| | | ecstasy | E | Henry | H |
| caught | C | energy | E | holy man | ST |
| church | CH, CE | engineers | RE | hospital | H |
| | | English | E | hot | H |
| circle | O | European | E | hour(s) | H, HR |
| clubs | C | exercises | PE | | |

| husband | H | name | N | sailor | AB |
|---------|---|------|---|--------|-----|
| | | navy | RN | saint | ST |
| in charge | IC | navy | N | second(s) | S |
| inspector | DI | new | N | secretary | PA |
| iron | FE | noon | N | ship | SS |
| | | North(ern) | N | silver | AG |
| Jack | J | | | small | S |
| | | old | O | society | S |
| King | K, R | one | A, I | soft(ly) | P |
| kiss | X | outsize | OS | soldier | GI |
| knight | K | over | O | son | S |
| | | oxygen | O | south(ern) | S |
| large | L | | | spades | S |
| learner | L | page | P | square | S |
| left | L | painter | RA | stone | ST |
| Liberal | L | parking | P | street | ST |
| line | L | penny | P, D | succeeded | S |
| lines | LL | piano | P | | |
| litre | L | politician | MP | theologian | DD |
| loud | F | pound | L | time | T |
| love | O | power | P | ton(s) | T |
| | | pressure | P | Tory | CON |
| maiden | M | | | | |
| male | M | queen | ER | university | U |
| mark(s) | M | question | Q, | | |
| married | M | | QU | very | V |
| masculine | M | quiet(ly) | P, SH | very loud | FF |
| mass | M | | | very quiet | PP |
| member | MP | races | TT | volume | V |
| mile | M | record | EP, | vote | X |
| million(s) | M | | LP | | |
| Mike | M | Republican | R | weight | W |
| minute(s) | M | resistance | R | west(ern) | W |
| monarch | ER, | right | R | wide | W |
| | R | ring | O | width | W |
| money | M | river | R | wife | W |
| Monsieur | M | road | RD | with | W |
| month | M | Romeo | R | work | OP |
| morning | AM | rook | R | | |
| motorway | M, | royal | ER | yard | Y |
| | MI | round | O | year(s) | Y |
| | | run(s) | R | zero | O |

## 2. Solutions: 120 Practice Clues

In the following two sections of annotated solutions, letters that form anagrams (anagram fodder), are shown by an asterisk, definitions are *italicised* and indicators are <u>underlined</u>.

### ANAGRAM CLUES

| | | |
|---|---|---|
| 1 | Shun bad <u>dancing</u> *partner*<br>**shun bad**\* | HUSBAND |
| 2 | *Lady* I rather <u>fancy</u><br>**I rather**\* | HARRIET |
| 3 | *Greens perhaps* <u>misrepresenting</u> Mao Tse-Tung<br>**Mao Tse Tung**\* | MANGETOUTS |
| 4 | Looks for brand <u>new</u> *UK holiday destination*<br>**looks for brand**\* | NORFOLK BROADS |
| 5 | *Adhesive* tapes <u>come unstuck</u><br>**tapes**\* | PASTE |
| 6 | Pope with trousers <u>off</u> – that's *unthinkable!*<br>**pope trousers**\* | PREPOSTEROUS |
| 7 | *Break down* after <u>moving letters</u> from close pal<br>**close pal**\* | COLLAPSE |
| 8 | Guests beginning to get <u>drunk</u> and *intimate*<br>**guests g**\* | SUGGEST |
| 9 | *Swallow* a mouth rinse <u>erroneously</u><br>**a mouth rinse**\* | HOUSE MARTIN |
| 10 | *Where one pays for the other* doorbell <u>to be fixed</u><br>**doorbell**\* | BORDELLO |

### SANDWICH CLUES

| | | |
|---|---|---|
| 1 | *It makes us take shelter* <u>in</u> centre of Boston?<br>**lee inside st** | SLEET |

| 2 | A half slice of cake _in_ peach _trifle_<br>**a gat(eau) inside belle** | BAGATELLE |
| 3 | _Dope_ left <u>in</u> bed<br>**l inside cot** | CLOT |
| 4 | Under <u>wraps</u> by _choice_<br>**per inside sub** | SUPERB |
| 5 | Record <u>held by</u> old Delta pilot flying for _so long_<br>**record = EP inside o D pilot\*** | TOODLEPIP |
| 6 | _Shock treatment_ I <u>received in</u> Harley St in error<br>**I inside Harley St\*** | HAIRSTYLE (shock of hair) |
| 7 | Terrible rip _in_ chair? _I see what you're saying!_<br>**rip\* inside leader** | LIP READER |
| 8 | <u>Casually dressed</u> newspaperman _stopped by police_<br>**Ed inside pullover** | PULLED OVER |
| 9 | _Little girl_, one _in_ a hundred<br>**I inside L L = 100** | LIL |
| 10 | _Container_ ship's contents <u>secured by</u> mate<br>**hi inside pal** | PHIAL |

**HOMOPHONE CLUES**

| 1 | _Rent_ going up, <u>it's said</u> | HIRE (higher) |
| 2 | _Post_ for a man, <u>so to speak</u> | MAIL (male) |
| 3 | _Praises_ cricket's HQ <u>on the radio</u> | LAUDS (Lord's) |
| 4 | Naked lady <u>reported</u> in _Indian city_ | NEW DELHI (nude Ellie) |
| 5 | _Flood_ covering Florence <u>spoken of</u> | OVERFLOW (over Flo') |
| 6 | <u>Audibly</u> one affected by illness in _chest_ | COFFER (cougher) |
| 7 | _Ways_ to get to Greek island <u>broadcast</u> | ROADS (Rhodes) |

| 8 | <u>Reportedly</u> start race for *a pudding* | SAGO (say go) |
| 9 | *Hard stuff* in barracks <u>by the sound of it</u> | BOOZE (boos) |
| 10 | *M Easterner* in pub, wet <u>one's heard</u> | BAHRAINI (bar rainy) |

## TAKEAWAY CLUES

| 1 | <u>Cut</u> price *rum* <br> **price = odds minus s** | ODD |
| 2 | Heresy meets with motion of approval? <u>Not</u> here! <br> **heresy minus here + nod** | SYNOD |
| 3 | Toilet seat <u>not</u> half *wobbly* <br> **loo + seat minus at** | LOOSE |
| 4 | First <u>off</u> most harsh *mountain* <br> **severest minus s** | EVEREST |
| 5 | WW1 enemy <u>destroying</u> British *missile launch site* <br> **Boche minus B** | OCHE |
| 6 | *It's painful* <u>extracting</u> penny from sporran <br> **pouch minus p** | OUCH |
| 7 | Flying Gulf Air, one <u>goes</u> for *Economy* <br> **Gulf air\* minus I** | FRUGAL |
| 8 | Trouble brewing over <u>missing</u> *murder suspect* <br> **trouble\* minus o = over** | BUTLER |
| 9 | Doing housework <u>ignoring</u> initial *inclination* <br> **cleaning minus c** | LEANING |
| 10 | Perhaps stupidly hospital's <u>gone</u> *private* <br> **perhaps \* minus H** | SAPPER |

## HIDDEN CLUES

| 1 | Peer <u>in</u> Thro**ne Ro**om for *King* | NERO |

| 2 | *Pack he'd lead* <u>regularly</u> | AKELA |
|---|---|---|
| 3 | *Brickbats* <u>in part</u> o**f lak**e | FLAK |
| 4 | *Food item* <u>eaten by</u> **v**e**gg**ies? | EGG |
| 5 | <u>Sample of</u> Niv**ea's tender s**kin *soap* | EASTENDERS |
| 6 | *Sauce* requiring <u>a bit of</u> chil**li p**owder | LIP |
| 7 | <u>Some</u> tarm**ac cra**cks in *African city* | ACCRA |
| 8 | *Uniform* <u>packed and folded</u> by hous**emas**ter | SAME |
| 9 | *Fish* ha**te tra**wler <u>nets</u> | TETRA |
| 10 | Hä**agen-Da**zs <u>retains</u> this *secret plan* | AGENDA |

**REVERSAL CLUES**

| 1 | *Does perhaps* rush <u>around</u> <br> **rush = reed** | DEER |
|---|---|---|
| 2 | Bear <u>up</u> – here's *a ring* <br> **Bear = Pooh** | HOOP |
| 3 | *Put out* by <u>mounting</u> objections <br> **objections = buts** | STUB |
| 4 | *Some privates* <u>reversed</u> positions <br> **position = set twice** | TESTES |
| 5 | *Type of car* to sell <u>back</u> <br> **sell = flog** | GOLF |
| 6 | A medic <u>repelled</u> by *appendix* <br> **a medic = a doc** | CODA |
| 7 | *Dull* poet <u>recalled</u> <br> **poet = bard** | DRAB |
| 8 | Huge flans <u>all round</u> – that's the *trick!* <br> **mega tarts** | STRATAGEM |
| 9 | *Look* in hold <u>on the way back</u> <br> **hold = keep** | PEEK |
| 10 | <u>Reversed</u> slump in *US fuel* <br> **slump = sag** | GAS |

## LETTER SWITCH CLUES

1   Left <u>to replace</u> inner parts of Tchaik-
    ovsky *score*
    **went replacing inside of
    Tchaikovsky**                                    TWENTY

2   *Do* a <u>heart transplant</u> for Tom
    **he-cat with c moved forward**                  CHEAT

3   *What grass is, even <u>for</u> a fool*
    **e'en replacing ass in grass**                  GREEN

4   *Highest priest*'s story – <u>the last shall
    be first</u>
    **story = lie with switch of letters**           ELI

5   *One taking legal action* regrets <u>switch-
    ing sides</u>
    **rues becoming suer**                           SUER

6   *Orderly* Helen <u>changing direction</u> in
    bed
    **L becoming R in Helen**                        COHERENT

7   *Scorn* from MP <u>replacing</u> second in
    contest
    **MP replacing s = second in contest**           CONTEMPT

8   *Dance* a litle time, last couple <u>swap-
    ping places</u>
    **minute with last two letters
    exchanged**                                      MINUET

9   *Miss* drunken binge, one <u>coming in for</u>
    a different one
    **piss-up becoming pass up**                     PASS UP

10  *Like the web?* Ladies have a <u>change</u> of
    heart
    **women with v replacing m**                     WOVEN


## ALL-IN-ONE CLUES

1   *Over fifty? <u>Wrong!</u>*
    **over fifty***                                  FORTY-FIVE

| 2 | *Setting forth?* <u>About</u> *right* | STARTING |
| | **r inside stating = setting forth** | |
| 3 | *Join a navy* <u>initially</u> *as this?* | SEAMAN |
| | **seam + a n** | |
| 4 | <u>Reverse of</u> *fine and cool?* | NAFF |
| | **f = fine + fan = cool reversed** | |
| 5 | *Result of endless spree in which a lot* <u>is</u> <u>drunk</u>*?* | BLOATING |
| | **a lot\* inside bing (e)** | |
| 6 | <u>Not normally seen</u> *in UK bars!* | BURKAS |
| | **UK bars\*** | |
| 7 | *What's displayed on iPhone,* <u>extremely</u> *large?* | APPLE |
| | **app + l(arg)e** | |
| 8 | <u>Fantastic</u> *crowd puller?* <u>Not half!</u> | WORLD CUP |
| | **crowd pul(ler)\*** | |
| 9 | <u>Take part in</u> *rulin**g** **o**ver **n**ation* | GOVERN |
| | **hidden clue** | |
| 10 | *We will* <u>get excited</u> *with Ring seats* | WAGNERITES |
| | **we Ring seats\*** | |

### DOUBLE DEFINITION CLUES

| 1 | *Mad passionate lovers* | BONKERS |
| 2 | *One photographing a crocodile* | SNAPPER |
| 3 | *Just get the hell out of here!* | LEGIT |
| 4 | *Herb is a man's name* | BASIL |
| 5 | *Honest ie not lying* | UPRIGHT |
| 6 | *Don't hit girl!* | MISS |
| 7 | *A Greek starter* | ALPHA |
| 8 | *Rhubarb crumble* | ROT |
| 9 | *White pawn* | HOCK |
| 10 | *Press club* | IRON |

## ADDITIVE CLUES

1. *Clever person* packed underwear
   **bra in box**
   BRAINBOX

2. *Member of family* has information on us
   **gen + us**
   GENUS

3. What arrives as August ends? A *touch of colour*
   **Sep 1 + A**
   SEPIA

4. Small beds for *Highlanders*
   **s + cots**
   SCOTS

5. An examination *of Chambers*
   **a trial**
   ATRIAL

6. Call at the start before surgery gets *busy*
   **c + op, busy = detective**
   COP

7. Maiden cheated? *That's by no means rare!*
   **over + done**
   OVERDONE

8. *Skilful* ace, the opposite of gauche
   **A + droit**
   ADROIT

9. *Hooded killer* from Royal Horse Artillery
   **King + cob + RA**
   KING COBRA

10. Quiet English *girl*
    **sh + E**
    SHE

## CRYPTIC DEFINITION CLUES

1. *Hamburger's first-class?*
   KINDERGAR-TEN

2. *Pig that flies!*
   GANNET

3. *Writer gradually worn down on A4?*
   PENCIL

4. *Hairdresser's perk?*
   FRINGE BENEFIT

5. *What I must be when small*
   DOTTED

| 6 | *They have two legs and fly* | TROUSERS |
| 7 | *Man United playing away from home* | ADULTERER |
| 8 | *Lunch for a cowardly balloonist?* | CHICKEN IN A BASKET |
| 9 | *A pound of sultanas* | HAREM |
| 10 | *This cylinder is jammed* | SWISS ROLL |

## NOVELTY CLUES

| 1 | *Happen to get 200 in 45 minutes!*<br>**CC in our (75% of hour)** | OCCUR |
| 2 | *Two and six in old money*<br>**2 + 6 = 8** | PIECES OF EIGHT |
| 3 | *Cut off – not dat limb, though!*<br>**dis member** | DISMEMBER |
| 4 | *Program advising accomodation changes?*<br>**accommodation misspelled** | SPELLCHECKER |
| 5 | A swan, deprived of space, sits on *this river*<br>**Join A to swan** | ASWAN |
| 6 | Nothing squared is *something cubed*<br>**o times o** | OXO |
| 7 | *InterCity?*<br>**inter and city** | BURY |
| 8 | *Works for Foreign Office wet?*<br>**FO + undry** | FOUNDRY |
| 9 | *Not having IOU? Aye*<br>**all the vowels** | VOWELLESS |
| 10 | Sunderland *docks*<br>**s under land** | LANDS |

# 3. Solutions: 24 Practice Puzzles

## Puzzle 1: The Sun

**Across**

1 Theatre tutor's *old means of transport*
   **additive**
   STAGECOACH – stage coach

8 *It does beat vegan food*
   **double definition**
   PULSE

9 Increases desire, that's *swell*
   **additive**
   UPSURGE – increases = ups + desire = urge

10 Pa's <u>about</u> to pull up on *the road surface*
   **additive incl anagram**
   ASPHALT - pas* + pull up = halt

11 *Anchors* on *open heaths*
   **double definition**
   MOORS

12 *Pull towards a body* when Vi a target <u>maybe</u>
   **anagram**
   GRAVITATE – Vi a target*

15 *Shades of colour sound qualities*
   **double definition**
   TONES

17 A builder, <u>nearly crazy</u>, *can be heard*
   **anagram incl takeaway**
   AUDIBLE – a builde(r)*

19 Be a star <u>performing</u> *side by side*
   **anagram**
   ABREAST – be a star*

20 I love <u>stewed</u> *fruit*
   **anagram**
   OLIVE – I love*

21 *Final attempt* to endure holiday town
   **additive**
   LAST RESORT – last + resort

**Down**

2 *Bulb* <u>surprisingly</u> lit up
   **anagram**
   TULIP – lit up*

3 A danger <u>is crushed</u> in *Caribbean island*
   **anagram**
   GRENADA

4 *Risk total defeat at Wimbledon?*
   **cryptic definition**
   COURT DISASTER

5 *Tea* for fool in the morning
   **additive**
   ASSAM – fool = ass + a.m.

6 Moorhen <u>desperately</u> seeking *adrenaline, perhaps*
   **anagram**
   HORMONE – moorhen*

7 *Small county where people go to retire?*
   **double definition**
   BEDS

8 <u>Hear</u> dog in *summit*
   **homophone**
   PEAK – sounds like peke

12 *Universal soldier*
   **double definition**
   GENERAL

13 A dour <u>disposition</u> you and I

found *wearying*
**additive incl anagram**
ARDUOUS – a dour* + you
and I = us

14 *At this point* in **t**he **re**hearsal
**hidden**
HERE

15 Qui**te a k**nack <u>keeping</u> *timber*

**hidden**
TEAK

16 *Difficulties* with small horses
**additive**
SNAGS – small = s + nags

18 British air <u>ruined</u> *wild rose*
**additive incl anagram**
BRIAR – British = Br + air*

---

## Puzzle 2: Daily Mail

**Across**

1 *Influential condition Elgar
noted with pomp*
**double definition**
CIRCUMSTANCE

8 *Edited* and *prepared for examination*
**double definition**
REVISED

9 *Unsold stock* to support
record
**additive**
BACKLOG – back + log

11 Article men <u>rewrite</u> *relating
to trade*
**anagram**
MERCANTILE – article
men*

12 Young animal with one
*chrysalis*
**additive**
PUPA – pup + a

14 *Type of swine* a danger <u>run-
ning around</u> middle of pen
**sandwich incl anagram**
GADARENE – (p)e(n) inside a
danger*

16 *Old Spanish change* put <u>into</u>
plant
**sandwich**

PESETA – set inside pea

17 **Grant**'s <u>regular</u> *gun*
**hidden**
GAT – G( r)a(n)t

19 *Show off* Florida relative
**additive**
FLAUNT – FL + aunt

21 *Confine* remainder at court,
<u>keeping</u> Irish <u>back</u>
**sandwich incl reversal**
RESTRICT – Ir(ish) reversed
in rest + Ct

24 *Source of energy* at home
when he <u>quits</u>
**takeaway**
ATOM – at (h)om(e)

25 Speak once (<u>badly</u>) <u>about</u>
good *old birthday treat*
**sandwich incl anagram**
SPONGE CAKE – g inside
speak once*

27 Mark <u>grabs</u> money, *a lasting
power*
**sandwich**
STAMINA – M inside stain + a

28 *Knot* <u>resolved</u> in daring <u>cut
with</u> middle of sword
**sandwich incl anagram**
GORDIAN – (sw)o(rd) inside
daring*

29 *US docker* <u>rearranged</u> organs on helm
**anagram**
LONGSHOREMAN – organs on helm*

**Down**

1 Vicar <u>turns up in</u> mixed school *with hat on*
**sandwich incl reversal**
COVERED – Rev reversed inside Coed

2 *Rarest tuna* <u>cooked</u> here?
**all-in-one anagram**
RESTAURANT – rarest tuna*

3 It's more expensive going out *modernising*
**additive**
UPDATING – up + dating

4 Bust <u>smashed</u> by the Parisian's *hard to detect*
**additive incl anagram**
SUBTLE – bust* + le

5 *Expert's* rare <u>in</u> a church
**sandwich**
ARCH – r inside a Ch

6 *Conspire* – lines by Unionist <u>put into</u> cipher
**sandwich**
COLLUDE – ll + U inside code

7 <u>Fancy</u> farm foie gras? *It'sthick and creamy*
**anagram**
FROMAGE FRAIS – farm foie gras*

10 *Promising* rain-gauge's <u>working about</u> ten <u>maybe</u>
**sandwich incl anagrams**
GUARANTEEING – ten* inside raingauge*

13 *Beat it*; English races went ahead in <u>rising</u> gloom
**sandwich incl reversal**
KETTLEDRUM – E TT + led inside murk reversed

15 <u>*Essential part of cereals, crushed*</u>
**all-in-one hidden incl anagram**
EAR – (ce)rea(ls)*

18 Generate <u>broadcast</u> for *someone in second decade*
**anagram**
TEENAGER – generate*

20 <u>Head off</u> chaos at a party *of green hue*
**additive incl takeaway**
AVOCADO – (h)avoc + a do

22 I get <u>stuck into</u> <u>translating</u> a Latin *language*
**sandwich incl anagram**
ITALIAN – I inside a Latin*

23 *Prominently display* Spanish whip
**additive**
SPLASH – Sp(anish) + lash

26 *Faction*'s victory over government
**additive**
WING – win + G

..........................................................................................................................

**Puzzle 3: Guardian – Rufus**

**Across**

1 *Range* of company found by MP on a ship
**additive**

COMPASS – Co + MP + a + SS

5 *Not quite a heavyweight vessel?*
**double definition**
CRUISER

9 *Bulb* lit up, when switched
**anagram**
TULIP – lit up*

10 I made case out for *specialised schools*
**anagram**
ACADEMIES – I made case*

11 *The constitution should be all the better for them*
**cryptic definition**
AMENDMENTS

12 A student is after an alternative *exam*
**additive**
ORAL – or + a + L

14 *It may have a good nap on the flight*
**cryptic definition**
STAIR CARPET

18 *Person with two hips?*
**cryptic definition**
CHEERLEADER

21 Some harbour dues *with which Indians are conversant*
**hidden**
URDU

22 *Break away from the craft*
**cryptic definition**
SHORE LEAVE

25 *Exacting examinations, involving litmus papers?*
**cryptic definition**
ACID TESTS

26 *One has to be what one is*
**cryptic definition**
OWNER

27 Sending out *terminations*
**anagram**
ENDINGS – sending*

28 *Getting fed up about midday?*
**cryptic definition**
AT LUNCH

**Down**

1 A yacht capsized in Old China
**anagram**
CATHAY – a yacht*

2 *Striker* appears satisfied about everything
**sandwich**
MALLET – all inside met

3 Ida strips a rampant *evergreen*
**anagram**
ASPIDISTRA – Ida strips a*

4 Around morning she gets a *feeling of guilt*
**sandwich**
SHAME – AM inside she

5 *Accountant may be after this* three-card trick
**anagram**
CHARTERED – three-card*

6 *Takes advantage*, gaining three points on centre court
**additive**
USES – (co)u(rt) + SES (compass points)

7 *Footholds on the mount*
**cryptic definition**
STIRRUPS

8 *Determined* to give poor Rose an instrument
**additive incl anagram**
RESOLUTE – Rose* + lute

13 Container to list in *aircraft manoeuvre*
**additive**

BARREL ROLL – barrel +
roll

15 <u>Sort out</u> that messy *collection
of stones*
**anagram**
AMETHYSTS – that messy*

16 *Precise* bill supported by a
junior minister
**additive**
ACCURATE – a/c + curate

17 *It's a blow that has to be faced*
**cryptic definition**
HEADWIND

19 Girl <u>came in</u> to study *the
weapon*

**sandwich**
CANNON – Ann inside con

20 *Want* to <u>disguise</u> hatred
**anagram**
DEARTH – hatred*

23 *A follower of Ethiopian emperor* and a Russian emperor
<u>uplifted</u>
**reversal**
RASTA – a Tsar reversed

24 Heads <u>up</u> to deliver *a knockout blow*
**reversal**
STUN – nuts reversed

## Puzzle 4: Financial Times – Falcon

**Across**

1 Obvious method *actors may
be seen here in Manhattan*
**additive**
BROADWAY – broad + way

5 Piece of silk? Look at *a sample*
**additive**
SWATCH – s(ilk) + watch

9 *Devious* sappers in charge
**sandwich**
INDIRECT – RE inside indict

10 A French child in Germany -
it's *cruel*
**additive**
UNKIND – un + kind (Ger-
man)

12 *Fortunate*, girl <u>receiving</u> king
**sandwich**
LUCKY – K(ing) inside Lucy

13 *Ivy, maybe, always growing*
**cryptic definition**
EVERGREEN

14 *Layout* of garrison <u>entered by</u>
graduate
**sandwich**
FORMAT – MA inside fort

16 *Dutch scholar*, helping to
make op**eras, mus**icals
**hidden**
ERASMUS

19 Each side, initially, on pitch
is *made up of famous players*
**additive**
ALL-STAR – all + s(ide) +
tar

21 *Rock* of Gibraltar's third
visited by a sailor
**additive**
BASALT – (Gi)b(raltar) + a salt

23 *Talk* in nightclub? Sure,
<u>when drunk</u>
**additive incl anagram**
DISCOURSE – disco + sure*

25 *What a bishop may wear in a
joint*

**double definition**
MITRE

26 New weapon, *restricted*
**additive**
NARROW – n + arrow

27 Ankle was <u>broken</u> in *ballet*
**anagram**
SWAN LAKE – ankle was*

28 *Written message* from *land-lord*'s in *character*
**triple definition**
LETTER

29 One-time collier <u>penning</u> article for *paper*?
**sandwich**
EXAMINER – a inside ex-miner

**Down**

1 *Check* back of veil <u>worn by</u> groom's partner
**sandwich**
BRIDLE – l inside bride

2 *The traditional type from Harrow, for example*
**cryptic definition**
OLD SCHOOL

3 Dry It <u>in cocktail</u> is *nasty*
**anagram**
DIRTY – dry It*

4 A new European coin <u>em-bodying</u> one that's *very old*
**additive incl sandwich**
ANCIENT – I inside a n + cent

6 Saw single <u>storm-tossed</u> *schooner, say*
**anagram**
WINEGLASS – saw single*

7 *Junk food*
**double definition**

TRIPE

8 *Pleasure-seeker*, male lectur-er, is sort of square
**additive**
HEDONIST – he + don + is + T

11 *Lake* shim**mere**d <u>somewhat</u>
**hidden**
MERE

15 *Device that marks time* – encountered no more, <u>strangely</u>
**additive incl anagram**
METRONOME – met + no more*

17 *Early form of transport*
**cryptic definition**
MILK TRAIN

18 Lie <u>about filming</u> a <u>naughty</u> nude in *colour*
**sandwich incl reversal and anagram**
EAU DE NIL – a + nude* inside lie reversed

20 *Seldom seen underdone*
**double definition**
RARE

21 *Polish* insects get larger
**additive**
BEESWAX – bees + wax

22 Nothing <u>in</u> measuring device can show *a shooting star*
**sandwich**
METEOR – o inside meter

24 *Fish* in <u>foreign</u> parts
**anagram**
SPRAT – parts*

25 *Note* that goes <u>up or down</u>
**reversal**
MINIM

## Puzzle 5: Daily Telegraph

**Across**

1 *Skill* <u>fixing</u> fence, if icy
**anagram**
EFFICIENCY – fence if icy*

6 *Bound to leave*
**double definition**
SKIP

9 *Vehicles*, vehicles – <u>about</u> time!
**sandwich**
CARTS – t in cars

10 Select Poe <u>works</u> *to shorten*
**anagram**
TELESCOPE – select Poe*

12 Old bishop and minister in *study*
**additive**
OBSERVE – o + B + serve

13 Rushed for instance <u>towards the West</u>'s *diversity*
**additive incl reversal**
RANGE – ran + eg reversed

15 *Agitated* conductor leading band's climax
**additive**
RATTLED – Rattle + ban(d)

17 Former lover suggested getting *bare*
**additive**
EXPOSED – ex + posed

19 *Country* retreat with distinguishing characteristic
**additive**
DENMARK – den + mark

21 *Hearing* sounds <u>back</u>, son must be <u>captivated</u>
**sandwich incl reversal**
SESSION – s in noises reversed

22 Model of car and every *train*
**additive**
TEACH – (Ford model)T + each

24 *Business* skill <u>returned</u>: very loudly in charge
**additive incl reversal**
TRAFFIC – art reversed + ff + i/c

27 *Keeping* in power <u>involved keeping</u> quiet
**sandwich incl anagram**
OWNERSHIP – sh inside in power*

28 *Say* nothing <u>in</u> sin
**sandwich**
VOICE – O in vice

29 Holy man, the old *thing that's painful to see around*
**additive**
STYE – St + ye

30 *Fired up*, <u>50 per cent of</u> encounters were angry
**additive incl takeaway**
ENCOURAGED – en-cou(nters)+ raged

**Down**

1 <u>Branch of</u> sw**eet ch**estnut's *cut*
**hidden**
ETCH

2 Catch <u>up</u> after pro got *left behind*
**additive incl reversal**
FORGOTTEN – for + got + net reversed

3 *Charges* people from the Highlands leading southern <u>moves</u>?
**letter switch**
COSTS – Scots with initial S moved to centre

4 *Went in* hospital department before daughter
**additive**
ENTERED – ENT + ere + d

5 Company suggest <u>leaving</u> a *place of learning*
**additive incl takeaway**
COLLEGE – Co + (a)llege

7 *Recognised* **kin**d *of* **wi**ne <u>regularly taken out</u>
**hidden**
KNOWN

8 *Putting on an act* before start of theatrical finale
**additive**
PRETENDING – pre + t + ending

11 *What person in the Navy could want* rubbish <u>on board</u> ship?
**sandwich**
STRIPES – tripe in SS

14 *Customs* raid – it's not <u>unusual</u>
**anagram**
TRADITIONS – raid its not*

16 Mad king <u>wielding</u> the *whip* sandwich
LEATHER – the inside Lear

18 *Some tailors initially longing to finish this?*
**all-in-one additive**
STITCHING – s(ome) t(ailors) + itching

20 Thick <u>stews</u> in French *cuisine, <u>as they say in Paris</u>*
**additive incl anagram**
KITCHEN – thick* + en

21 *Head cleaner* has mop <u>bent</u> over
**additive incl anagram**
SHAMPOO – has mop* + o

23 Refusal <u>to tuck into</u> any *bug*
**sandwich**
ANNOY – no inside any

25 Female continually creating *state of excitement*
**additive**
FEVER – f + ever

26 *Heroic exploit*, <u>whichever way you look at it</u>
**reversal**
DEED

.................................................................................

**Puzzle 6: Oxford Times – Colin Dexter**

**Across**

1 *Joint cover – not comprehensive though*
**cryptic definition**
LOINCLOTH

6 Party Mr Heath *loved excessively*
**additive**
DOTED – do + Ted (Heath)

9 *Sweet* Jane? Name first with Tarzan
**additive**
FONDANT – (Jane) Fonda + n + T

10 *Rein? Initially, no colt <u>could be without</u>* it
**all-in-one sandwich incl anagram**
CONTROL – r inside no colt*

11 *Plants* do, <u>in</u> Channel Islands

sandwich
CACTI – act in CI

12 *Job in which you could make lots of brass*
**cryptic definition**
METALWORK

13 *Northampton Town FC are rubbish!*
**double definition**
COBBLERS

15 *One's weak – one to get a PM cross?*
**all-in-one additive incl reversal**
WIMP – w + I + PM reversed

19 *Spirit shown by Mand**ela** (**N**elson)*
**hidden**
ELAN

20 *Bane, this, if much drunk*
**all-in-one anagram**
ABSINTHE – bane this*

23 *Posh crockery – present for the old Dutch*
**cryptic definition**
DELFTWARE

24 Spy one *shark here, maybe?*
**additive**
BONDI – Bond + I

26 *Half-bike whizzed with pace around part of Delhi?*
**all-in-one sandwich incl anagram**
PEDICAB – D inside bi(ke) pace*

27 *They flutter etc. – mostly timid*
**all-in-one anagram incl takeaway**
TITMICE – etc timi(d)*

28 *Sort of mush to bed Umbelliferae at first*
**all-in-one sandwich incl**

anagram
HUMUS – U inside mush*

29 *Quietly in love with rest? The outcome, perhaps*
**all-in-one sandwich incl anagram**
OVERSLEPT – p inside love rest*

**Down**

1 *Bio-system peddled, it's said, in Health Shop*
**novelty incl homophone**
LIFECYCLE – sounds like pedalled

2 *Like column in a Palladio niche?*
**partial all-in-one hidden**
IONIC

3 *Quack's shouldering responsibility, if it's broken*
**cryptic definition**
CLAVICLE

4 *How to be cleverer? O, must work with skill*
**anagram**
OUTSMART – O must* + art

5 *Divine Power from the Catechism*
**hidden**
HECATE

6 *Bradman's famous duck*
**double definition**
DONALD

7 It's shocking to embrace wrongdoing: *that's him though, to a "T"*
**additive**
TERRORIST – error inside it's* + T

8 Drink in Denmark *is automatically controlled*

**sandwich**
DALEK – ale in DK

14 <u>Twist</u> made bold <u>about</u> second helping of meat? *This stopped that*
**sandwich incl anagram**
BEADLEDOM – (m)e(at) inside made bold*

16 *Bush-whackers criticize the new one?*
**cryptic definition**
PRESIDENT – George Bush

17 Tease Ben <u>cruelly</u>, but *one is not ticked off*
**anagram**
ABSENTEE – tease Ben*

18 *With which best idea is <u>to get treatment</u>*

**all-in-one anagram**
DIABETES – best idea*

21 *A lot* of hay
**double definition**
STACKS

22 *If one's shooting, aim for panda!*
**cryptic definition**
BAMBOO

23 *In the main, such a charge is damaging*
**cryptic definition**
DEPTH

25 *Feature <u>surrounding</u> one always at disco*
**partial all-in-one sandwich**
NOISE – I in nose

---

## Puzzle 7: The Oldie – Antico

Thematic down answers 10 and 20: AUTUMN LEAVES

### Across

7 *Discover* doctor <u>in</u> control
**sandwich**
RUMBLE – MB inside rule

8 *Commemoration* <u>returning</u> each year, <u>in</u> essence, after end of parade
**additive incl sandwich & reversal**
EPITAPH – (parad)e + p.a reversed in pith

11 *Top* combination <u>in</u> university assignment
**sandwich**
UPPERMOST – perm inside U post

12 *Searches for favourite places*

**two definitions per theme**
H(A)UNTS

13 Time yet to be <u>abandoning boundaries</u> with new *change of policy*
**additive incl takeaway**
U-TURN – (f)utur( e) + n

15 *Purity* <u>corrupted</u> once <u>inside</u> pub before church
**additive incl sandwich & anagram**
INNOCENCE – once* inside inn + CE

17 Negative reponse by letter, <u>out of order</u>, <u>not using</u> right *item of stationery*
**additive incl anagram and takeaway**
NOTELET – no + lette( r)*

19 *Contemporary* work, one

about <u>filling</u> time left
**sandwich**
TOPICAL - op + I + ca inside t l

21 Puss <u>stopped by</u> road beside
fit *place for nap?*
**additive incl sandwich**
CARD TABLE - rd inside cat
+ able

23 *Policeman* taking a trail <u>back</u>
**reversal**
GARDA - a drag reversed

24 *Tap side of cut gem*
**two definitions per theme**
FA(U)CET

26 *Be drawn,* <u>endlessly</u> critical,
<u>into</u> scrape
**sandwich incl takeaway**
GRAVITATE - vita(l ) in grate

28 Price put up for *daub*
**additive**
SPLODGE - (starting) price =
SP + lodge

29 *Gives out pieces of absorbent
paper*
**two definitions per theme**
(T)ISSUES

**Down**

1 *Clear* hesitation with magistrate <u>around</u>
**sandwich**
JUMP - um inside JP

2 Serious, <u>first off</u>, about *king*
**additive incl takeaway**
OBERON - (s)ober + on

3 *One after pleasure* in hold-up
<u>plugged by</u> crime boss
**sandwich**
HEDONIST - Don inside heist

4 *Groom left at end of meal?*
**two definitions per theme**
(U)NEATEN

5 Near agreement, <u>raised</u> *drink
at bedtime*
**additive incl reversal**
NIGHTCAP - nigh + pact
reversed

6 *Story* b**y** v**a**gr**a**nt <u>with odd
bits cut out</u>
**hidden alternate letters**
YARN

9 Son <u>admitted to</u> loathing *hurry*
**sandwich**
HASTE - s inside hate

14 *Thorough grumble*
**two definitions per theme**
(M)UTTER

16 <u>Some</u> macaro**ni cer**tainly
*more agreeable*
**hidden**
NICER

18 Line on bird <u>penned by</u> poet
<u>lacking finish</u> and *freedom*
**additive incl sandwich &
takeaway**
LATITUDE - l + tit inside
Aude(n)

19 Tact I <u>managed</u>, <u>skirting</u>
edge *of subject*
**sandwich incl anagram**
THEMATIC - hem inside tact I*

21 *Hits,* latest in music, very
loud <u>in</u> America
**additive incl sandwich**
CUFFS - (musi)c + ff inside US

22 *Incompetent producer of taps*
**two definitions per theme**
BU(N)GLER

23 Good to get over anger,
<u>catching</u> second *salmon*
**additive incl sandwich**
GRILSE - g + s inside rile

25 *Collected* part of engine <u>bro-
ken by</u> learner

**sandwich**
CALM – L inside cam

27 *Declare* answer and <u>upset</u>

vicar
**additive incl reversal**
AVER – A + Rev reversed

---

## Puzzle 8: Sunday Times – Tim Moorey

**Across**

1 *Courage not available – poor deliveries*
**double definition**
NO BALLS

5 F Field and B Silver in *run-down hotel*
**additive**
FLEABAG – F + lea + B + Ag

9 One remains <u>to occupy</u> post in *water plant*
**sandwich**
MARE'S TAIL – a rest inside mail

10 Learner <u>inside</u> just showing *style*
**sandwich**
FLAIR – L inside fair

11 *Island holiday*
**double definition**
EASTER

12 *Private* parking near <u>New</u> Orleans
**additive incl anagram**
PERSONAL – P + Orleans*

14 *Fruit* celebrity requests one's <u>overlooked</u>
**additive incl takeaway**
STAR APPLES – star appl(I)es

16 Mug <u>returned</u> and *put down*
**reversal**
LAID – dial reversed

18 Newlywed <u>not good</u> in *kitchen perhaps*
**takeaway**
ROOM – (g)room

19 *Laughing a lot as one may be on leaving theatre*
**cryptic definition**
IN STITCHES

22 <u>After rough handling</u> Roget did get *worn out*
**anagram**
DOG-TIRED – Roget did*

23 William gets love? *A lot if like this!*
**additive**
BILLY-O – Billy + love = O

26 *Basket producer* the**re is o**nly <u>backed in part</u>
**hidden reversal**
OSIER

27 *Get garage <u>rebuilt</u> and you may need this*
**all-in-one anagram**
AGGREGATE – get garage*

28 *Bums* are <u>held back</u> in clothes
**sandwich incl reversal**
TOERAGS – are reversed inside togs

29 *I defy you* to give boozer present
**additive**
SO THERE – sot + here

**Down**

1 *Book* for *anaesthetists?*
**double definition**
NUMBERS

2 *Mugs* from *a county*

---

**double definition**
BERKS

3 *City* girl <u>hanging around</u> star
**sandwich**
LAS VEGAS - Vega inside lass

4 Feeling of humiliation <u>most-ly</u> *false*
**takeaway**
SHAM - sham (e)

5 *Plates* <u>can be represented</u> as the feet <u>around</u> Bow in London
**sandwich incl anagram**
FALSE TEETH - L inside as the feet*

6 <u>Short on top</u>, egotistical and *mischievous*
**takeaway**
ELFISH - (s)elfish

7 *Condition* of lingerie at the laundry!
**additive**
BRAINWASH - bra in wash

8 Uniform line by journalist *confused*
**additive**
GARBLED - garb + l + Ed

13 Cadge a lot in *bathroom containers*
**additive**

SPONGE BAGS - sponge + bags

15 <u>Rogue</u> dealing so *close to a bank?*
**anagram**
ALONGSIDE - dealing so*

17 Second missile is *urgent*
**additive**
STRIDENT - s + Trident

18 *Endure* southern resort <u>mentioned?</u> Unacceptable
**additive incl homophone**
RIDE OUT - sounds like Ryde + out

20 *Language* being <u>taken up?</u> Nothing <u>in it</u>
**sandwich incl reversal**
SLOVENE - love inside ens reversed

21 *This is evidently the first and last in* **s**aloon car**s**
**novelty**
SIERRA - Saloon carS

24 *Let* pound drop a bit
**additive**
LEASE - L + ease

25 *Potential birdies, maybe eagles*
**cryptic definition**
EGGS

---

## Puzzle 9: Observer – Everyman

### Across

1 *See* vine tangled with herb
**additive incl anagram**
ENVISAGE - vine* + sage

5 *Abandon thread*
**double definition**
STRAND

9 *Covered* past life initially with relief
**additive**
OVERLAID - over + l(ife) + aid

10 *Is painful* technique <u>used in</u> texting?

**sandwich**
SMARTS – art inside SMS

12 *Environmentalist's signal to proceed*
**double definition**
GREEN

14 *Custom immune to criticism* from airman blushing <u>aboard</u> boat
**sandwich**
SACRED COW – AC red inside scow

15 Propose measure before social gathering for *indoor game*
**additive**
TABLE FOOTBALL – table + foot + ball

17 *Certainly* sense hot <u>excitement of</u> bout, duo <u>receiving</u> cheers
**additive incl sandwich and anagram**
WITHOUT A DOUBT – wit + H + ta inside bout duo*

21 Resistance <u>in</u> territory by soldier, cold and *calculated*
**sandwich**
STRATEGIC – R inside state + GI + C

22 *Greek character* <u>absorbed by</u> argument he tackled
**hidden**
THETA

23 *License* book <u>in revolutionary</u> electronic way
**sandwich incl reversal**
ENABLE – b inside E lane reversed

24 *Unlucky* one, round <u>in</u> valley, <u>in retreat</u>
**additive incl sandwich**

**and reversal**
ILL-FATED – I + fat inside dell reversed

26 Thirsty <u>to grab</u> attention? *Not interesting*
**sandwich**
DREARY – ear inside dry

27 *Linguistic unit* <u>in translation of</u> sly label
**anagram**
SYLLABLE – sly label*

## Down

1 *Stretch*, with energy left, operating barrier
**additive**
ELONGATE – E + l + on + gate

2 *Struggle* with <u>unfinished</u> scene
**takeaway**
VIE – vie(w)

3 *Quiet* because <u>occupied by</u> French article
**sandwich**
SILENCE – le inside since

4 *Artist* captures nobody's heart? Harsh
**additive**
GAINSBOROUGH – gains + (no)bo(dy) + rough

6 *Paint* moderate area
**additive**
TEMPERA – temper + a

7 Curtail urge <u>to reform</u> *land management*
**anagram**
AGRICULTURE – curtail urge*

8 *Deny any connection* with inspector, planted
**additive**

DISOWN – DI + sown
11 English clubs still followed by supporter *very happily*
   **additive**
   ECSTATICALLY – E + C + static + ally
13 Inclination, <u>changing</u> gear, <u>to cut</u> extra *hard work*
   **sandwich incl anagram**
   ELBOW GREASE – bow + gear* inside else
16 Trio, <u>not half oppressed by</u> burden, *cross*
   **sandwich incl takeaway**
   STRADDLE – tr(io) inside saddle

18 *Gossip* time after time <u>going into</u> story? Right
   **sandwich**
   TATTLER – t t inside tale + r
19 *Responsible* university scientist finally <u>separating new</u> fluid
   **sandwich incl anagram**
   DUTIFUL – U (scientis)t inside fluid*
20 *Move up* when around goal
   **additive**
   ASCEND – as + c + end
25 *Clumsy boat* yet <u>to capsize</u>
   **reversal**
   TUB – but reversed

........................................................................................

## Puzzle 10: The Week – Tim Moorey

### Across

1 *What Australians make wine from*
   GRIPES
4 Service veteran *manipulated figures*
   **additive**
   MASSAGED – mass + aged
10 *Traffic jam*
   AUTOCUE
11 *Concorde*
   EXPLAIN
12 *Euphoric* greeting <u>heard</u>
   **homophone**
   HIGH – sounds like hi
13 Croatian resort calls for *key holders*
   **additive**
   SPLIT RINGS – Split + rings
15 *Toast by the Queen*
   CHAIRS
16 *Woman from Finland*

FINESSE
20 *To stop stopping*
   DECEASE
21 Juliet say, <u>mostly</u> getting *highly addictive drug*
   **takeaway**
   HEROIN – heroin (e)
24 Nurses <u>seen around</u> coral island with *religious leaders*
   **sandwich**
   AYATOLLAHS – atoll inside ayahs
26 *Public protest* in Delaware and Missouri
   **additive**
   DEMO – DE + MO
28 *Nonsense spoken by taxi-drivers*
   CABBAGE
29 *One who has reached the age of consent*
   CANTEEN

30 *Unnecessary* sharp pointers
   succeeded initially
   **additive**
   NEEDLESS – needles + s(uc-
   ceeded)
31 *Someone who is coughed upon*
   COFFEE

## Down
1 Number <u>missing</u>, chap rings
   <u>out</u> for *computer images*
   **anagram incl takeaway**
   GRAPHICS – chap ri(n)gs*
2 *Answer to question: Where's
   t' coal?*
   INTEGRATE
3 *Engrave* <u>two thirds</u> of rough
   drawing
   **takeaway**
   ETCH – (sk)etch
5 *Cockney dentures*
   APERITIF
6 <u>Badly</u> depressed <u>about</u> university and get *displaced*
   **sandwich incl anagram**
   SUPERSEDED – U inside
   depressed*
7 Elderly relative <u>consumes</u>
   one *cereal*
   **sandwich**
   GRAIN – I inside Gran
8 *Sweet pastry* one's <u>seen in</u>
   bowl

sandwich
DANISH – an inside dish
9 *Times* casual worker looking
   down on one
   **additive**
   TEMPI – temp + I
14 *Wide-ranging discussion
   costing nothing?*
   **double definition**
   FREE-FOR-ALL
17 A softened <u>composition</u>? *No
   good for one such*
   **anagram**
   STONE-DEAF – a softened*
18 What's added at the end
   changes *liturgical books*
   **additive**
   PSALTERS – PS + alters
19 *28 grams*
   ANNOUNCE
22 *Tintin's partner*
   CAN-CAN
23 Sun journalist in *roughly
   built hut*
   **additive**
   SHACK – Sun = S + hack
25 Blame <u>invalid</u> for *a slow walk*
   **anagram**
   AMBLE – blame*
27 *Data* <u>from</u> ra**in-fo**rest
   **hidden**
   INFO

## Puzzle 11: Sunday Telegraph

### Across
1 *Kind of ball* fashioned <u>around</u>
   square, <u>oddly</u>
   **sandwich incl anagram**
   MASQUERADE – square*

inside made
6 *Appear* in place of bishop,
   taking mass
   **additive**
   SEEM – see + m(ass)

9   *HQ for force* in *Waterloo, say*
    **double definition**
    STATION

10  *Poke fun at* a politician <u>in</u> flier
    **sandwich**
    LAMPOON – a MP inside loon

12  *Attractive* urgent <u>coverage for</u> legal support team
    **sandwich**
    PREPOSSESSING – posse inside pressing

14  *Surfing, maybe* at equator
    **additive**
    ONLINE – on + line

15  *PC, for example,* <u>frantically</u> cut rope <u>binding</u> maiden
    **sandwich incl anagram**
    COMPUTER – M inside cut rope*

17  Former partner having case for *enforcement of payment*
    **additive**
    EXACTION – ex + action

19  <u>In</u> w**ar, can a**ccept *things being kept secret*
    **hidden**
    ARCANA

22  Group of swimmers before the race <u>upset</u> *instructor*
    **additive incl anagram**
    SCHOOLTEACHER – school + the race*

24  Academic <u>penning</u> papers *is tiresome*
    **sandwich**
    DRAGS ON – rags inside don

25  Clubs make certain *statement attributing blame*
    **additive**
    CENSURE – C + ensure

26  *Home for nocturnal creature*

fixed ahead of time
**additive**
SETT – set + t

27  *Have second thoughts about* condition <u>covering</u> European disadvantages
    **sandwich**
    RECONSIDER – E + cons inside rider

## Down

1   *Get engaged* repeatedly <u>in</u> sche**mes Ho**l**mes h**atched
    **hidden**
    MESH – hidden twice

2   *It's used for opening act in theatre*
    **cryptic definition**
    SCALPEL

3   *Global organisation* <u>badly</u> tainted <u>within</u> alliances
    **sandwich incl anagram**
    UNITED NATIONS – tainted* inside unions

4   Organised party membership, initially *unsystematic*
    **additive**
    RANDOM – ran + do + m

5   Study <u>about</u> soul I <u>misrepresented</u> in *error*
    **sandwich incl anagram**
    DELUSION – soul I* in den

7   *I'll feature prominently in his speech*
    **cryptic definition**
    EGOTIST

8   *Like those in charge,* chap set over African country <u>shifting</u> left
    **additive incl letter switch**
    MANAGERIAL – man + Algeria, L moved to end

11 *Doesn't understand* I'm <u>upset</u>, perhaps <u>wrongly</u>, over aims
**additive incl reversal and anagram**
MISAPPREHENDS – I'm reversed + perhaps* + ends

13 *Serious type*, in this way, also <u>embracing</u> monarch
**additive incl sandwich**
SOBERSIDES – so + R inside besides

16 *Carry on* once unit is <u>given new order</u>
**anagram**
CONTINUE – once unit*

18 <u>Put</u> the "A" <u>in</u> art, *essentially*
**sandwich**
AT HEART – the A inside art

20 *On the rocks, possibly* needing silver bullet
**additive**
AGROUND – Ag + round

21 <u>Cut short</u> awkward old *cowboy*
**additive incl takeaway**
GAUCHO – gauch( e) + o

23 <u>It sounds like</u> sweetheart *does, for instance*
**homophone**
DEER – sounds like dear

.............................................................

## Puzzle 12: Independent on Sunday – Hoskins

**Across**

1 *Mess that an angler might have had a hand in?*
**double definition**
CAN OF WORMS

6 You could say I am good <u>about</u> *clothes*
**reversal**
GARB – brag reversed

10 A <u>brief</u> dram plus Bud – that's *living*
**additive incl takeaway**
ANIMATE – a ni(p) + mate

11 *Nasty complaint* <u>impeding</u> cavity? Bend <u>over</u>!
**sandwich incl reversal**
CHOLERA – hole in arc reversed

12 *Did this*, being annoyed <u>about</u> wife
**sandwich**
SWORE – w inside sore

13 *Amazed* to see One Direction having fight
**additive**
AWESTRUCK – a + west + ruck

14 *Get out of it*, perhaps with individual on Bass
**additive**
BEGONE – B + eg + one

16 *Slips away* from area and sleeps <u>around</u>
**anagram**
ELAPSES – area = a sleeps*

18 Time Her Maj <u>should enter</u> a service *sober*
**sandwich**
AUSTERE – t + ER inside a use

21 *Incidents in the 100 and 200 metres?*
**double definition**
EVENTS

24 I'd neither <u>gone off</u> or *was left*

**anagram**
INHERITED – I'd neither*

25 In flagrante, but <u>half-upset</u>
(cold *room*)
**additive incl reversal**
ATTIC – at + it reversed + c

26 *Half-pint* of cider taken regularly after whisky?
**additive**
SHORTIE – short + ie

27 *Beast* always chasing after
flushed duke
**additive**
RED DEER – red d + e'er

28 <u>Having changed</u> top, bother
*to work out?*
**letter switch**
SUSS – fuss with switch of S
for F

29 <u>Cook</u> did entrées, then
*pounded the meat?*
**anagram**
TENDERISED – did entrees*

**Down**

1 *Rough* business heading
waste disposal unit?
**additive**
COARSE – Co + arse

2 I'm soon <u>dancing</u> on E and
*awfully smelly*
**additive incl anagram**
NOISOME – I'm soon* + E

3 *Stitch up* celebrity <u>cut by</u>
Republican leader
**sandwich**
FRAME – R inside fame

4 *Work* and work with energy
on speed
**additive**
OPERATE – op + E + rate

5 Teach me *to fly* a *chopper in*
the jungle?
**anagram**
MACHETE – teach me*

7 *Ways* a love goddess <u>will
inspire</u> ecstasy
**sandwich**
AVENUES – E inside a Venus

8 *Salty* bishop <u>cut twice</u> is
<u>full of</u> anguish
**sandwich incl takeaway**
BRACKISH – rack inside
Bish(op)

9 Hint of a strangler *in Danny
Dyer's face*
**additive**
BOAT RACE – boa trace and
cockney slang

15 Extra charge *to put May in
the good PM category?*
**additive**
OVERRATE – over + rate

17 What completes Liam of
Oasis: <u>wrestling</u> *dons?*
**anagram**
MAFIOSOS – (Lia)m of Oasis*

19 *German building* kit**sch**,
**loss**-making <u>houses</u>
**hidden**
SCHLOSS

20 *Intense*, but <u>unopened</u> message about Hoskins
**additive incl takeaway**
EXTREME – (t)ext + re + me

21 Stop, you ruddy *bore*
**additive**
ENDURED – end + U (text
messaging) + red

22 *Are they a bit higher than
belly laughs?*
**cryptic definition**
TITTERS

23 So <u>lacking in love</u>, my editor

*bought drugs*
**additive incl takeaway**
SCORED – s(o) + my = cor
+ Ed

25 *Summer* days <u>in embrace of</u> a
European Romeo
**sandwich**
ADDER – d d inside a E R

···································································

## Puzzle 13: The Times – Unnamed

**Across**

1 *Scraps in a shower after match*
**cryptic definition**
CONFETTI

6 *Got* staff <u>back in</u> case of blockage
**sandwich incl reversal**
BECAME – mace reversed inside b(lockag)e

9 *Snow* still <u>coming from the east</u>
**reversal**
NEVE – even reversed

10 Plunder left *misery*
**additive**
SPOILSPORT – spoils + port

11 *Leaves* flight with first team
**additive**
STEPS ASIDE – steps + A-side

13 After <u>second-half switch</u>, many *confused*
**letter switch**
LOST – lots, last two letters changing places

14 Tube list <u>for commuting</u> *displayed translation*
**anagram**
SUBTITLE – tube list*

16 *Rather silly* how the Queen is represented
**additive**

INANER – in an ER

18 *Rest* on slopes <u>after a set-back</u>
**additive incl reversal**
SPIDER – re + dips reversed

20 *American* finding room to work in between areas a lot <u>reduced</u>
**additive incl sandwich and takeaway**
ALABAMAN – lab inside a a + man(y)

22 *Who might get caught <u>for</u> parking in area for vegetables?*
**all-in-one letter switch**
CLOT – plot with C replacing P

24 *Key* for a disappointed officer?
**Additive**
A-FLAT MAJOR – a + flat + major

26 *Amphibian* say, <u>lacking</u> stern and <u>seen in</u> the sea near Calais
**additive incl takeaway and sandwich**
SALAMANDER – sa(y) + and inside la mer

28 *Periods of time* <u>mostly</u> put out of one's mind
**takeaway**
ERAS – eras(e)

29 *Curse* <u>flipping</u> metal having

a screw loose
**reversal**
DAMN IT – tin + mad reversed

30 Possible advice from Walton for this *musical accompaniment?*
**additive**
CASTANET – cast a net (Izaak W; author of Compleat Angler)

**Down**

2 <u>Wanting introductions</u>, veiled and dowdy woman *to use a superior club?*
**additive incl takeaway**
OVERTRUMP – veiled = (c)overt + dowdy woman = (f)rump

3 *Shabby place* bound <u>to be shown in</u> correspondence
**sandwich**
FLEAPIT – leap inside fit

4 Back of court seat <u>originally</u> providing *cover for a seed*
**additive incl anagram**
TESTA – (cour)t + seat*

5 Response ministers get in *artificial language*
**additive**
IDO – I do (wedding service)

6 Bare all in <u>dancing</u>? *I wouldn't do that!*
**anagram**
BALLERINA – bare all in*

7 Crown singer Fitzgerald *a star*
**additive**
CAPELLA – cap + Ella

8 *Customs* needing extra staff initially
**additive**
MORES – more + s(taff)

12 Face <u>rocks in</u> unfavourable *part of Everest?*
**sandwich incl anagram**
ICE FALL – face* inside ill

15 *Rent* wrong <u>around</u> Californian valley meeting resistance
**additive incl sandwich**
TORN APART – Napa + R inside tort

17 *Complex* lecture supporting European party
**additive**
ELABORATE – E Lab + orate

19 Keep <u>belting</u> runs and *leave coach behind*
**sandwich**
DETRAIN – r inside detain

21 Not a strong attorney in *the Spanish way*
**additive**
ALAMEDA – a lame DA

23 Fix <u>up</u> with a *climber*
**additive incl reversal**
LIANA – nail reversed + a

25 *Starts* tea <u>for an audience</u> with appropriate vessels
**additive incl homophone**
TURNS – t (sounds like tea) + urns

27 *Quack* comes from duck <u>confined by</u> US district
**sandwich**
DOC – O inside DC

## Puzzle 14: The Times Quick Cryptic – Dazzler

**Across**

1 *In Australia a capital* idea and deal that's <u>extraordinary</u>
**anagram**
ADELAIDE – idea deal*

5 *Dessert* made by wife with it
**additive**
WHIP – wife = w + with it = hip

8 Fellow <u>boxing</u> minute *title-holder*
**sandwich**
CHAMP – minute = m inside chap

9 *Effectiveness* of company shown by data extremely clearly
**additive**
COGENCY – Co + gen + c(learl)y

11 Feel airport <u>needs changing</u> *to grow rapidly*
**anagram**
PROLIFERATE – feel airport*

13 US author to judge *verse*
**additive**
POETRY – Poe + try

14 *Complete* current book and part of play
**additive**
INTACT – current = I + book = NT + act

17 Boy accompanying Queen twice is *a Casanova*
**additive**
PHILANDERER – Phil + and + ER ER

20 Famous authoress <u>with no name</u> on *grave*
**additive incl takeaway**
AUSTERE – Austen less name = n + on = re

21 *Group of revolutionary activists* with duke <u>in</u> charge
**sandwich**
CADRE – duke = D in care

22 *American* is *a jerk*
**double definition**
YANK

23 Traveller always <u>recalled carrying</u> one *spare*
**additive incl reversal and sandwich**
REPRIEVE – rep + I in ever reversed

**Down**

1 *Knowing* military music <u>hasn't started</u>
**takeaway**
ARCH – (m)arch

2 *Model* partner once generous
**additive**
EXAMPLE – ex ample

3 *Take illegally? Right*
**double definition**
APPROPRIATE

4 Nothing that is *dear*
**additive**
DUCKIE – nothing = duck + ie

6 *Dye* hard girl <u>picked up</u>
**additive incl reversal**
HENNA – H + Anne reversed

7 Nasty MEP <u>fiddled</u> *allowances*
**anagram**

PAYMENTS - nasty MEP*
10 *Market trader perhaps* is inexperienced and rather vulgar, <u>we hear</u>
**additive incl homophone**
GREENGROCER - green + grosser = grocer
12 Curate finally happy in <u>re-stored</u> *church festival*
**anagram**
EPIPHANY - (Curat)e happy in*
15 Cross written at bottom of a *contract*
**additive**

ABRIDGE - a + cross vb = bridge
16 *Stick* lands <u>regularly</u> at this spot
**additive incl hidden**
ADHERE - (l)a(n)d(s) + here
18 *Playwright* identified by <u>some</u> li**nes bi**tterly <u>upset</u>
**hidden reversal**
IBSEN - inside lines bitterly reversed
19 *Garden party* making fortune <u>reportedly</u>
**homophone**
FETE - sounds like fate

........................................................

## Puzzle 15: The Times Quick Cryptic - Joker

### Across

1 Severely criticise left for *understanding*
**additive**
RAPPORT - rap +left = port
5 *Wrong* a young lady
**additive**
AMISS  a + miss
8 <u>Nearly all</u> rib coach for *filter on entry to the cup*
**additive incl takeaway**
TEA-STRAINER - teas(e) + trainer
10 *Region* <u>of</u> F**ar Ea**st
**hidden**
AREA
11 Conservative's initial whipping leads to *arguing*
**additive**
CLASHING - C + lashing
12 *Recent* milky espresso needs sugar, ultimately

**additive**
LATTER - latte + (suga(r)
14 *Who deals with ship's hold* or deck when <u>working</u>
**anagram**
DOCKER - or deck*
16 Train too <u>awkward</u> for *turning round*
**anagram**
ROTATION - train too*
18 Beginning to produce beer *with little colour*
**additive**
PALE - p + ale
20 *One who asked for more* fruit takes right new treatment
**additive**
OLIVER TWIST - olive + right = r + twist
22 Process of colouring material <u>without</u> energy is *failing*
**takeaway**

DYING – dy(e)ing

23 Written as poetry *upside down*
   **additive**
   INVERSE – in verse

## Down

2 *Change* of flag that's <u>not the first</u>
   **takeaway**
   ALTER – (f) alter

3 Game bird <u>losing</u> head to horrible *farm worker*
   **takeaway**
   PEASANT – p(h)easant

4 *What one doesn't like to be discovered* <u>in</u> **trat**toria?
   **hidden all-in-one**
   RAT

6 *Artist* – one <u>from</u> Bavarian capital
   **takeaway**
   MUNCH – Mun(i)ch

7 *Unusual* stone found on top of a series of hills
   **additive**
   STRANGE – stone = st + range

9 A group on *leave*
   **additive**
   ABANDON – a band + on

11 Wow! Lovely *ornamental moulding*
   **additive**
   CORNICE – wow = cor + nice

13 A game with generally hollow *defence*
   **additive**
   APOLOGY – a polo + g(ener-all)y

15 *Fancy* limit being put on staple food
   **additive**
   CAPRICE – limit = cap + rice

17 *Foreign sci-fi film*
   **double definition**
   ALIEN

19 *Sacred water lily* louts <u>destroyed</u>
   **anagram**
   LOTUS – louts*

21 *One hundred mph* – never <u>going over</u>
   **reversal**
   TON – never = not reversed

## Puzzle 16: The Times Quick Cryptic – Orpheus

### Across

1 Church member <u>entertaining</u> a *top boxer, perhaps*
   **sandwich**
   CHAMP – a in ch member = MP

4 <u>Report of</u> district that's *more breezy*
   **homophone**
   AIRIER – sounds like area

9 *Italian physicist*'s <u>brief</u> month on island?
   **additive**
   MARCONI – Marc(h) + on + I

10 Old railwaymen given points *to look after*
   **additive**
   NURSE – NUR (former rail union) + S E (compass points)

11 *Uproar* in <u>first half</u> of meal
**takeaway**
DIN – din(ner)

12 Her deli's <u>output</u> is *greatly enjoyed*
**anagram**
RELISHED – her delis*

15 *Obliging, acting as a landlord?*
**double definition**
ACCOMMODATING

17 *Tear* delicate fabric, meeting cost
**additive**
LACERATE – lace + cost = rate

18 Bachelor originally attending tennis *club*
**additive**
BAT – bachelor = B + a(t-tending) t(ennis)

20 *Old England cricketer's elegance of manner?*
**double definition**
GRACE

22 *One with no illusions* about a register
**additive**
REALIST – about = re + a list

23 *Remove* obstruction <u>in</u> river
**sandwich**
DELETE – obstruction = let inside Dee

24 <u>Unusually</u> regal *composer*
**anagram**
ELGAR – regal*

**Down**

1 *Entertainer*'s scam <u>involving</u> TV, press etc
**sandwich**
COMEDIAN – media inside scam = con

2 In favour of <u>wearing</u> a new *pinafore?*
**sandwich**
APRON – pro inside a new = n

3 *Broadcast* made by expert with very little weight
**additive**
PROGRAMME – pro + gramme

5 *Pub* that's popular: Nag's Head
**additive**
INN – popular = in + Nag's Head = N

6 *Like Ben-Gurion*, head <u>off</u> British prime minister
**takeaway**
ISRAELI – (D)israeli

7 Genuine-<u>sounding</u> *Scottish dance*
**homophone**
REEL – sounds like real

8 *Rich person*'s factory, one on Yorkshire river
**additive**
MILLIONAIRE – factory = mill + one = I + on Aire

13 Unoriginal friend's *impasse in chess*
**additive**
STALEMATE – unoriginal = stale + mate

14 *Rabble-rouser* finally appearing at a riot, <u>unhappily</u>
**anagram**
AGITATOR – (appearin)g at a riot*

16 *French painter* left to support tea girl
**additive**

CHAGALL – tea = cha + gal
+ l
18 Old crooner <u>accepts</u> pound
for *flashy jewellery*
**sandwich**
BLING – pound = l in Bing
(Crosby)
19 A good press chief *much
advanced in years*

**additive**
AGED – a good = g + press
chief = Ed
21 *Tailed amphibian* familiar at
first <u>in</u> sci-fi film
**sandwich**
EFT – familiar at first =
f inside ET

---

## Puzzle 17: The Times Quick Cryptic – Grumpy

**Across**

1 *Tough guys* <u>breaking</u> ribs?
Sure!
**anagram**
BRUISERS – ribs sure*

5 Like one with a *large landmass*
**additive**
ASIA – as + I + a

9 Queen follows favourite *saint*
**additive**
PETER – pet + ER

10 A word <u>we hear in a German
accent</u>? So it's *alleged*
**homophone**
AVERRED – sounds like a
word!

11 *Cooler* that is cold <u>inside</u>
**sandwich**
ICE – c inside ie

12 *Proposed* name I don't
<u>change</u>
**anagram**
NOMINATED – name I
don't*

13 I'm <u>taken aback</u> by anger?
That's *an illusion*
**additive incl reversal**
MIRAGE – Im reversed + rage

15 Sibling <u>ignoring</u> the second

*disturbance*
**takeaway**
BOTHER – b(r)other

17 Lorna's family has least
amount of data *to contribute*
**additive**
DO ONE'S BIT – (Lorna)
Doone's + bit

19 *Sprite* <u>seen in</u> hot**el f**oyer
**hidden**
ELF – in hotel foyer

20 Tie up an <u>awkward</u> *flower*
**anagram**
PETUNIA – tie up an*

21 *Confused when sailing?*
**double definition**
AT SEA

22 Mormon's end beside salt *lake*
**additive**
TARN – sailor = tar + (Mor-
mo)n

23 *Begin to understand* material
one <u>doesn't finish</u>
**additive incl takeaway**
COTTON ON – cotton + on(e)

**Down**

1 *Initiation* that's suitable is <u>in</u>
British Museum

**sandwich**
BAPTISM – suitable = apt is
inside BM

2 Family member <u>doesn't start</u>
*to let loose*
**takeaway**
UNTIE – (a)untie

3 Jump on places for putting
*veg*
**additive**
SPRING GREENS – spring +
places for putting = greens

4 *Province* in actual centre of
Germany
**additive**
REALM – actual = real +
(Ger)m(any)

6 *Withdraw from minor injury*
**double definition**
SCRATCH

7 *Extra* snake <u>almost</u> died
**additive incl takeaway**
ADDED – adde(r) + died = d

8 *Simple dish* – not as snob ate

<u>in mess</u>
**anagram**
BEANS ON TOAST – not as
snob ate*

14 *Cock* Robin initially <u>waving</u>
to Rose
**additive incl anagram**
ROOSTER – R + to rose*

16 *Hold back* from *the chorus*
**double definition**
REFRAIN – two meanings

17 Extremely desirable drug
*store*
**additive**
DEPOT – d(esirabl)e + pot

18 *Encouraging word* for *Charlie's predecessor*
**double definition**
BRAVO – Charlie in NATO
alphabet

19 <u>Uncommon</u> sense in *a German city*
**anagram**
ESSEN – sense*

## Puzzle 18: The Times Quick Cryptic – Marty

**Across**

1 Alec stands <u>waving</u> *something on the beach*
**anagram**
SANDCASTLE – Alec
stands*

8 *Offer comfort to* Tory only
**additive**
CONSOLE – Con + sole

9 <u>Some backing</u> from f**air
Am**erican *girl*
**hidden reversal**
MARIA

10 *Jolly experience with LSD?*

**double definition**
TRIP – jolly (noun)

11 <u>Rudely</u> jeer any English *novel*
**anagram**
JANE EYRE – jeer any E*

13 *Expelled* school inspectorate,
<u>making one change</u>
**letter switch**
OUSTED – OFSTED with U
for F

14 *Entices* office workers? <u>About</u>
time
**sandwich**
TEMPTS – t inside temps

17  Raw treat <u>prepared</u> for *am-phibious rodent*
    **anagram**
    WATER RAT - raw treat*
19  Wonderful <u>going round</u> foremost of night *spots*
    **sandwich**
    ACNE - n(ight) inside ace
21  D**o**es w**a**l**k**, s**a**y, <u>regularly</u> in *Japanese city*
    **hidden alternate letters**
    OSAKA
22  Minor quarrel to have in *Cheltenham?*
    **additive**
    SPA TOWN - spat + own
23  *Music hall song, unspecific request to golf caddie?*
    **double definition**
    ANY OLD IRON

## Down

2   Article completes the undo-ing of *relatives*
    **additive**
    AUNTIES - a + unties
3   Party, alternatively, provid-ing *means of escape?*
    **additive**
    DOOR - do + or
4   *Primate*'s name secretary <u>recalled</u>
    **reversal**
    APEMAN - name PA re-versed (- 's = is )
5   Be visibly embarrassed after little boy *beamed*
    **additive**
    TIMBERED - little boy =

Tim + be red
6   Nobleman years *ahead of his time?*
    **additive**
    EARLY - Earl + years = y
7   *Maybe Chinese* food at the back
    **additive**
    FAR EASTERN - fare + astern
8   *Protective material*, <u>designed</u> to cool, won't
    **anagram**
    COTTON WOOL - to cool wont*
12  *To prepare* vinta**ge, tread y**ear's <u>contents</u>
    **hidden**
    GET READY
15  Picture army officer with old *musical instrument*
    **additive**
    PICCOLO - pic + Col + o
16  *Young lady* <u>distributed</u> med-als
    **anagram**
    DAMSEL - medals*
18  *Jewelled headdress*: it <u>elevated</u> a painter
    **additive incl reversal**
    TIARA - it reversed + a + RA
20  *Garment* <u>starts off</u> **s**mall **a**nd **r**arely **i**ncreases
    **hidden**
    SARI

## Puzzle 19: The Times Quick Cryptic – Tracy

**Across**

1 Vessel behind heading for small *Channel island*
**additive**
SARK – small = s + ark

3 Pair watch, perhaps, for *unfaithful partner*
**additive**
TWO-TIMER – pair = two + watch = timer

9 First half of song softly managed by old *singer*
**additive**
SOPRANO – so(ng) + softly = p + ran + o

10 *Invalidate* yearbook, <u>removing</u> second article
**takeaway**
ANNUL – yearbook = annu(a)l

11 *Turn out to be* point ahead
**additive**
END UP – point = end + ahead = up

12 Good access for *aristocracy*
**additive**
GENTRY – good = g + access = entry

14 Hate it, a late TV <u>broadcast</u>, but *take no further action*
**anagram**
LEAVE IT AT THAT – hate it a late*

17 *Basic* piano <u>installed in</u> flat
**sandwich**
STAPLE – piano = p inside flat = stale

19 *Come back again* about aggressive dog
**additive**
RECUR – about = re + cur

22 *Crime* rendering rector <u>powerless</u>?
**takeaway**
ARSON – parson less p = power

23 *First sign*
**double definition**
INITIAL

24 *Dance* enthusiast <u>circling</u> with energy
**additive incl sandwich**
FANDANGO – with = and inside fan + energy = go

25 Supporting Democrat, *unelected President*
**additive**
FORD – for + Democrat = D

**Down**

1 *Kind, like a senior nurse?*
**double definition**
SISTERLY

2 *Quick* attack <u>trapping</u> leader of pack
**sandwich**
RAPID – p inside raid

4 *Daydreaming* in court, appearing before large assembly
**additive**
WOOL-GATHERING – court = woo + l + gathering

5 *Do exercises* in *school*
**double definition**
TRAIN

6 Rally <u>rounding</u> on *head of state*
**sandwich**
MONARCH – on in rally = march

7   *Function* of list, <u>reportedly</u>
    **homophone**
    ROLE – sounds like list = roll
8   *Specimen* provided by son,
    more than enough
    **additive**
    SAMPLE – son = s + ample
13  Set off, went out in front,
    *surprised*
    **additive**
    STARTLED – start + led
15  *Skilled worker* <u>from</u> Hob**art**
    **is a** **n**atural
    **hidden**
    ARTISAN
16  Go home and *go to bed*

    **additive**
    TURN IN – turn = go +
    home = in
18  *Herbivore* <u>filling</u> sauce**pan**,
    **da**ily
    **hidden**
    PANDA
20  Company <u>about</u> to broadcast
    in *capital*
    **sandwich**
    CAIRO – broadcast = air in
    Co
21  *Homeless child* **w**ould **a**ppear
    in **f**ront, <u>first of all</u>
    **hidden**
    WAIF – initial letters

---

## Puzzle 20: The Times Quick Cryptic – Howzat

### Across

4   <u>Irregular</u> dates happily in
    the end becoming a *regular
    one*?
    **additive incl anagram**
    STEADY – dates* + (happil)y
7   *Portrait* of Somalian <u>vandal-
    ised</u>
    **anagram**
    MONA LISA – Somalian*
8   *Countless* millions taken by
    milk producer <u>rejected</u>
    **additive incl reversal**
    MYRIAD – m + dairy re-
    versed
9   *Intimate* change and say
    nothing
    **additive**
    ALTER EGO – alter + eg + O
10  *Mean* singing voice <u>heard</u>
    **homophone**
    BASE – soumds like bass

12  *Pork cut* in box served with
    <u>processed</u> brie
    **additive incl anagram**
    SPARE RIB – box = spar +
    brie*
15  Quiet craftsman is *prejudiced*
    **additive**
    PARTISAN – p + artisan
18  *Quits flat*
    **double definition**
    EVEN
20  Sergeant <u>in mess</u> *put out of
    favour*
    **anagram**
    ESTRANGE – sergeant*
22  <u>Sounding</u> cold, *it's hot*
    **homophone**
    CHILLI – sounds like chilly
23  Good on imposing *French
    city*!
    **additive**
    GRENOBLE – g + re + noble

24 Cockney wife <u>having lost</u> capital, is after credit *support*
**additive incl takeaway**
CRUTCH – Cr + (d)utch

**Down**

1 *Dimwit* who is also *sweet*
**cryptic definition**
FOOL

2 *Sort of artist in a way associated with flags?*
**cryptic definition**
PAVEMENT

3 US soldier hires out *padded jackets*
**additive**
GILETS – GI + lets

4 Greek island associated with a *savoury snack*
**additive**
SAMOSA – Samos + a

5 Reh**ears**als <u>in part</u> for *organs*
**hidden**
EARS

6 *Due date that's not welcomed by caller?*
**double definition**

DEADLINE – dead line

11 *Secure* a time with TV presenter
**additive**
AT ANCHOR – a + t + anchor

13 Highest point <u>almost</u> for *pulse*
**takeaway**
PEA – pea(k)

14 *One way of getting to the top in say, Washington*
**cryptic definition**
ELEVATOR

16 *Seasonal transport* is murder, <u>one's heard</u>
**homophone**
SLEIGH – sounds like slay

17 *Madman* from northern state
**additive**
NUTTER – n + utter

19 *Scheduled time* for *opening*
**double definition**
SLOT

21 *Misses* prodi**gal s**on? <u>Not entirely</u>
**hidden**
GALS

....................................................................................

**Puzzle 21: The Times Quick Cryptic – Teazel**

**Across**

1 Selecting a ballad that's *cheap*
**additive**
GOING FOR A SONG – going for + a song

8 Underground <u>gets new head</u>, *consciously old-fashioned*
**letter switch**
RETRO – Metro changed to retro

9 *Amused* mark of approval

came first
**additive**
TICKLED – tick + led

10 Kitchen utensil, <u>I hear</u>, is *larger*
**homophone**
GREATER – sounds like grater

11 *Track down a tiny quantity*
**double definition**
TRACE

13 *Intended recipient* of notice sees red, <u>being replaced</u>
**additive incl anagram**
ADDRESSEE – notice = ad + sees red*

17 *Relatives* found in usual places, <u>commonly</u>
**takeaway**
AUNTS – (h)aunts (dropped aitch)

19 Travelled zigzag courses <u>as told</u>, *an imposition on driver*
**homophone**
ROAD TAX – sounds like rode tacks

20 *Unable to sail* in a grand circle
**additive**
AGROUND – a + G + round

22 *Body recently demoted* from place <u>ordered</u> out
**additive incl anagram**
PLUTO – place = pl + out*

23 *Mad not to be playing with nursery horse?*
**double definition**
OFF ONE'S ROCKER

**Down**

1 Say, a cloth <u>picked up</u> in *motor home*
**reversal**
GARAGE – eg a rag reversed

2 *Largely at sea*
**double definition**
IN THE MAIN

3 *Exulted*, told age <u>was wrong</u>
**anagram**
GLOATED – told age*

4 Subeditor here <u>corrected</u> "British Isles"
**anagram**
OUTER HEBRIDES – subeditor here*

5 A Hibernian *course*
**additive**
ASCOT – a Scot

6 <u>First off</u>, burn *fuel*
**takeaway**
OIL – (b)oil

7 Wander about to obtain *device*
**additive**
GADGET – gad + get

12 *Very afraid* weak crust <u>has collapsed</u>
**anagram**
AWESTRUCK – weak crust*

14 *Hair product*, counterfeit and low quality, <u>not finished</u>
**additive incl takeaway**
SHAMPOO – sham + poo (r )

15 *Tries* a drop <u>in</u> house
**sandwich**
HAS A GO – a sag inside house = ho

16 *Area of Somerset*, no longer low, with river?
**additive**
EXMOOR – ex + low (cattle) = moo + R

18 *Disdain* incentive, finally stubborn
**additive**
SPURN – spur + (stubbor)n

21 Concerned with following *man on the pitch*
**additive**
REF – concerned with = re + following = f

## Puzzle 22: The Times Quick Cryptic – Flamande

**Across**

1 Preserves link, <u>recruiting</u> English *spy*
**sandwich**
JAMES BOND – E inside preserves = jams + link = bond

6 Old boy <u>repulsed</u> by a *snake*
**additive incl reversal**
BOA – OB reversed + a

8 *Like a boy* left with his dad, <u>unusually</u>
**additive incl anagram**
LADDISH – left = L + his dad*

9 *Show off* volume by family member
**additive**
VAUNT – volume = v + aunt

10 Angelic, sober *sort, easy to spot*
**anagram**
RECOGNISABLE – angelic sober*

12 *Pamper* group on Greek island
**additive**
COSSET – Cos + set

13 *Social occasions* <u>welcomed</u> by prou**d ances**tors
**hidden**
DANCES

16 *Such perfect vision two decades into this century?*
**cryptic definition**
TWENTY-TWENTY – measure of perfect vision

19 *One doesn't like* <u>shifting</u> earth
**anagram**
HATER – earth*

20 Send society girl <u>back</u>, *now it's late evening?*
**reversal**
BEDTIME – emit deb reversed

22 *Nothing* i**n** mi**ll**, after <u>removal of</u> odd components
**hidden alternates**
NIL

23 Insignificant man on board *one evening after work?*
**additive**
WEEKNIGHT – wee knight

**Down**

1 *Girl* unwell after onset of jaundice
**additive**
JILL – onset of jaundice = j + ill

2 Finish <u>up interrupting</u> church service? That's *insane*
**sandwich incl reversal**
MADNESS – end rev inside mass

3 <u>Originally</u>, **s**ix **k**ilometres **i**mpossible for *runner in winter*
**hidden**
SKI

4 <u>Mostly</u>, one casual worker is *available*
**additive incl takeaway**
ON HAND – on( e) + casual worker = hand

5 *Destroy* borders of Delaware and Virginia, say
**additive**
DEVASTATE – DE + VA + state

6  Obscure book? *This descrip-*
   *tion might help*
   **additive**
   BLURB - obscure = blur +
   book = b

7  Recasts <u>failing</u> *performer*
   **anagram**
   ACTRESS - recasts*

11 *Defeat* leader of hecklers <u>in</u>
   public spat
   **sandwich**
   OVERTHROW - h inside
   overt row

12 *Understand how to become*
   *popular*
   **double definition**
   CATCH ON

14 *Press item causing offence*
   **double definition**
   CUTTING - two meanings

15 *Secure* small item of furniture
   **additive**
   STABLE - small = s + table

17 *Acclaim* former tax <u>reduced</u>
   by one pound
   **additive incl takeaway**
   EXTOL - ex + tol(l) pound = L

18 *Socialists abandoned side*
   **triple definition**
   LEFT - three meanings

21 *Lecturer* <u>seen in</u> Oxfor**d,**
   **on**ce
   **hidden**
   DON

...................................................................................................

## Puzzle 23: The Times Quick Cryptic – Hawthorn

**Across**

1  *Some heavy rain* for us after
   low pressure
   **additive**
   DOWNPOUR - low = down
   + p + our

5  *Spoils* of *war personified*
   **double definition**
   MARS

8  *Drink* large <u>rum</u>
   **anagram**
   LAGER - large*

9  M Escher, <u>perplexing</u> *creator*
   *of intricate designs?*
   **anagram**
   SCHEMER - M Escher*

11 *Vehicle* <u>parked in</u> Pennsyl**va-**
   **n**ia
   **hidden**
   VAN - in Pennsylvania

12 Rotten season for *the Cubs?*

   **additive**
   OFFSPRING - off = rotten +
   spring = season

13 *Word for scoundrel* to be
   announced <u>in</u> newspaper
   **sandwich**
   RATBAG - TBA inside rag

15 Adhesive <u>binding</u> agent: <u>rev-</u>
   <u>olutionary</u> *building material*
   **sandwich incl reversal**
   GYPSUM - agent = spy
   reversed in gum

18 <u>Destroyed</u> nicotine, <u>protect-</u>
   <u>ing</u> hearts *at risk*
   **sandwich incl anagram**
   ON THIN ICE - hearts = H
   in nicotine*

19 *Stick man*
   **double definition**
   ROD

20 Grandma <u>getting into</u> Dick-

ens, a *rewarding discovery*
**sandwich**
BONANZA – nan inside
Dickens = Boz + a
21 *Nation* state <u>rejecting</u> North
America
**takeaway**
INDIA – India(na)
22 Thanks company for *Mexican snack*
**additive**
TACO – ta + Co
23 *Plant* fake diamond?
**additive**
SHAMROCK – sham + diamond = rock

**Down**
1 <u>Take back</u> hated *present*
**reversal**
DELIVER – reviled reversed
2 *Cart* succeeded at <u>transporting</u> silver
**sandwich**
WAGON – silver = Ag inside
succeeded = won
3 <u>Prepared</u> point for ear *piercing*
**anagram**
PERFORATION – point for
ear*
4 Use fan <u>on the blink</u>? That's
*risky*
**anagram**
UNSAFE – use fan*
6 Tramp is <u>moving around</u>

smelly places?
**anagram**
ARMPITS – tramp is*
7 *Shoulder manoeuvre* <u>seen in</u>
Wel**sh rug**by
**hidden**
SHRUG
10 *Satisfactory compromise: one
likely to lift spirits?*
**double definition**
HAPPY MEDIUM
14 *Hugely powerful* <u>wrench</u> in
attic
**anagram**
TITANIC – in attic*
16 *Cosmetic treatment* getting
daughter and dad <u>covered in</u>
dirt
**sandwich**
MUDPACK – daughter = d +
dad = Pa inside dirt = muck
17 Hard day Inland Revenue
<u>turned up</u> for *capital*
**reversal**
RIYADH – hard = H + day +
IR all reversed
18 *Annual circulation in relation
to the Sun?*
**cryptic definition**
ORBIT – think solar system
19 Travelled over for *traditional
US event*
**additive**
RODEO – travelled = rode +
over = O

**Puzzle 24: The Times Quick Cryptic – Hurley**

**Across**
1 <u>In</u> Cara**cas sat a**waiting *ice
cream*

**hidden**
CASSATA
5 Exchange <u>involving</u> Mike's

*waterlogged area*
**sandwich**
SWAMP – Mike = M inside
exchange = swap

8  Defective seascapes clue?
   *These might give way out*
   **anagram**
   ESCAPE CLAUSES – sea-
   scapes clue*

9  *Complicated* time: old invader departs
   **additive**
   TANGLED – time = t + Angle
   + departs = d

10 Speaker's arguments for
   *ordinary writing*
   **homophone**
   PROSE – sounds like pros

11 Succeeded at first with aloof
   manner in *island*
   **additive**
   SICILY – s + icily

13 Somewhat re**tro ster**eo-
   typed *work list*
   **hidden**
   ROSTER

15 *Make changes* in plug fitting
   **additive**
   ADAPT – plug = ad + fitting
   = apt

16 *Agile* learner lives a bit
   **additive**
   LISSOME – L + lives = is + a
   bit = some

19 Well-known type of room for
   *water board?*
   **additive**
   PUBLIC UTILITY – public +
   utility

20 Left-winger returning with
   English *cake*
   **additive incl reversal**

TORTE – Trot reversed + E

21 *Difficult situation* of t**hro**a**t**y
   **Su**e, **p**as**t**y regularly
   **hidden alternate letters**
   HOT SEAT

## Down

1  Talk about energy *fraud*
   **sandwich**
   CHEAT – energy = E inside
   chat

2  Back Companion of Honour
   over warning colour in *House
   of Lords perhaps*
   **additive**
   SECOND CHAMBER – back
   = second + CH + amber

3  Dad upset over friend's *dismay*
   **additive incl reversal**
   APPAL – pa reversed + pal

4  Are gripping rascal in *shopping precinct*
   **sandwich**
   ARCADE – cad in are

5  *Soapy liquid* not what it
   seems, poor, ultimately
   lacking
   **additive incl takeaway**
   SHAMPOO – sham + poo( r )

6  The cartoonist upset, *having
   little advance warning*
   **anagram**
   AT SHORT NOTICE – the
   cartoonist*

7  *Pioneering chemist* super at
   broadcast
   **anagram**
   PASTEUR – super at*

11 *Refuse to leave* street? Indeed, sulk forgetting nothing
   **additive incl takeaway**

STAY PUT – St + indeed = ay + p(o)ut

12 Large upper room with Eastern *ornamental pattern* **additive**
LATTICE – large = L + attic + E

14 <u>Roughly</u> hustle *investigator* **anagram**

SLEUTH – hustle*

17 *Pole*'s second attempt to win **additive**
STILT – second = s + attempt = tilt

18 *Country* for example you passed through initially **additive**
EGYPT – eg + initial letters

## 4. Thanks

Above all, to Richard Heald for meticulously checking the whole text at the proof stage and before, often suggesting improvements using his unique and extensive crossword knowledge and skills. Richard also dealt patiently with my text conversion problems, especially as they meant his checking some parts twice.

To expert wordsmith Harvey Freeman who cast an experienced crossword eye over the whole text at a late stage and suggested many significant improvements, gladly accepted.

To Susie Bell, uncomplaining at my many mistakes, who typeset the book so efficiently and effectively.

To Mike Barker, Christopher Brougham and Colin Clarke for their help with specific issues.

To all the setters, named, pseudonymous or more often anonymous, whose puzzles and clues grace this book.

To crossword editors Colin Inman, Mike Hutchinson, Phil McNeill, Colin Gumbrell and Hugh Stephenson, whose approval to re-publishing was readily given.

To all at HarperCollins, especially Gerry Breslin who first suggested a generic book and saw it through to completion, greatly assisted by Michelle Fullerton.

Finally but by no means least, thanks to my wife Pamela for lots of wise advice and support, not just for this book, but for continuing to keep my teaching and speaking show on the road.

# Index

# THE ‌ TIMES

Shop the full range of Times Books from world-famous
atlases and puzzle books to Amazing Places and great lives –
there's something for everyone at timesbooks.co.uk.

ISBN: 978-0-00-829338-3
£150.00

ISBN: 978-0-00-826335-5
£25.00

ISBN: 978-0-00-828718-4
£16.99

ISBN: 978-0-00-822895-8
£14.99

ISBN: 978-0-00-826265-5
£9.99

Available to buy from all good booksellers and online.

www.timesbooks.co.uk          facebook.com/collinsref          @Collins_Ref

# THE  TIMES

Make every minute count with
The Times Quick Crossword books,
designed to stimulate the brain and hone
your general knowledge in the time it takes
to boil the kettle!

ISBN: 978-0-00-824129-2
£6.99

Available to buy from all good booksellers and online.

www.timesbooks.co.uk        facebook.com/collinsref        @Collins_Ref

# THE  TIMES

Do you find cryptic crosswords too much of a chore?
Do you want your general knowledge to be tested but
not put through the mill? The Sunday Times Concise
Crossword Book includes 100 crosswords, set out in a
clear, easy-to-use double-page spread to view layout,
plus all the solutions at the back of the book.

ISBN: 978-0-00-830089-0
£6.99

Available to buy from all good booksellers and online.

www.timesbooks.co.uk      facebook.com/collinsref      @Collins_Ref

# THE 🦁 TIMES

Whether you have five minutes to spare on your break or an entire Sunday morning with a cup of coffee, our range of Cryptic Crossword books are guaranteed to test your word power with over 100 world-famous cryptic crossword puzzles.

ISBN: 978-0-00-824130-8
£6.99

ISBN: 978-0-00-824128-5
£6.99

Available to buy from all good booksellers and online.

www.timesbooks.co.uk    **f** facebook.com/collinsref    🐦 @Collins_Ref